SUCCESS

&

SANITY

SUCCESS & SANITY

FINDING BALANCE, PEACE
AND PURPOSE IN A
PRESSURE-PACKED WORLD

TROY KORSGADEN

This book is dedicated to my mother, Iva Korsgaden.
She is, and always has been, my rock.

CONTENTS

CHAPTER 1 | THE BIG QUESTIONS

Well I've been to the mountain and I've been in the wind
I've been in and out of happiness
I have dined with kings, I've been offered wings
And I've never been too impressed.

—Bob Dylan[1]

I've lived a dream. By every measure of success, I've enjoyed more prosperity than any kid from a little California town ever should have expected, and I wouldn't trade a thing that has happened to me. It's been a wonderful ride. In the past few years, however, I've learned some new things that, like most of the important lessons in life, I discovered the hard way. They're invaluable to me, and I trust they'll be helpful to you, too.

Either/or. Many people in business and nonprofits, and even in the church world, have an unspoken (and most likely subconscious) assumption that a person can be either successful or sane, but not both. Everyone knows that anything valuable has a price tag, and success comes at a cost. That's true, but many leaders intuitively conclude that true success comes only at enormous sacrifice—of their families, their health, and even their sanity.

For much of my career, I climbed the peak of every goal and barreled through every obstacle to reach the top. People described me as driven, intense, and focused, and those adjectives are accurate. I knew what I wanted, and I went for it. I had a vision of success for the future that was so real I could taste it. I was completely focused on achieving my goals, and I never looked back. In fact, I seldom even looked to the side to see who was keeping pace with me. My fierce determination has been a large part of my success, but recently I've realized that I've paid too high a price.

We're not all the same. Many people in all kinds of companies and at all levels of their organizations are much like me, but others have drifted in the opposite direction. They were so committed to their families (or fishing or hiking or investments or golf or some other endeavor) that they neglected their work, and their careers suffered. Being out of balance can take many different forms, all of which are insidious and destructive.

All of us, the driven and the distracted, run the risk of missing the beauty of each moment. When we're at work, we're completely consumed with the next big goal we want to reach, or we daydream about being at home. And when we're at home, we're still thinking about a project at the office we didn't finish, or we dread the thought of going to work the next day. In all of these ways, we miss the joy of being in the moment, being "fully present" with each person, and celebrating every step they take.

I've always been focused on the future. When my mother tells people about my childhood, she often laughs. She explains that I would walk back and forth on the hearth of our fireplace talking to myself with obvious intensity: "I have to practice my piano so I can get better," or "I've lost my book, and I have to find it," or "I've got to get ready for my friend coming over." As my mother watched replays of this scene virtually every day, I'm sure she shook her head and smiled. Even as a young man, I was driven and focused.

I didn't change much when I went into business. I was always an innovator or an early adopter, on the front end of any new technology.[2] Using new technology, though, usually requires a learning curve. When fax machines were the newest rage, I immediately bought one for my office—the kind, you may remember, that used thermal paper. I sometimes took a faxed quote or another faxed paper from my office and put it in my car when I drove to meet with a client. On overcast days there was no problem, but if the sun was shining, the paper turned a horrible shade of brown or even black. I tried to shield the paper from the sun, but nothing worked. The paper became totally unusable.

In the early '90s, digital cellular "mobile phones" were becoming popular with business executives. Kids today have no idea how far the technology has advanced in only a few decades. Those of a certain age remember that those phones were more like suitcases with an antenna. We had to lug them everywhere we went, and the reception was only slightly better than being on Mars.

As technology became more sophisticated, the phone sizes got much more manageable. As my business really began to take off in 1990, I had the bright idea that I needed three cellphones: one for my agency, another for my consulting business, and a third for my family and personal life. It seemed like a perfect solution to keep those spheres compartmentalized—until two or all of the phones went off at the same time! I still have visions of myself jerking and thrusting hands into and out of multiple pockets, trying to answer all of them . . . and still sound cool and collected at the same time. I probably looked like I'd grabbed an electric wire! It's hard to sound confident and focused when you're trying to hold two or three conversations at the same time. The phones were a metaphor of my life: I was a whirlwind of activity, always chasing growth, success, and significance.

In recent years, however, I've crafted a radical, new definition of success—radical for me, at least. I used to wake up every day with a numerical target in mind, specific goals of new business, a number of a particular type of clients, or dollar amounts. In the insurance world, we talk about PIF (policies in force), and a wide range of different polices we offer our customers. Every industry and organization has its own metrics. The numbers aren't evil or wrong, but they're not the only things that are important. Now I see true success as a wonderful blend of peace and purpose. Peace of mind comes from giving each moment my best, being fully present with each person, and being more interested in others' success than my own. This peace means I don't have to beat myself up over the past, and I'm not so future-focused that I miss the present. But peace is only part of my new definition of success.

We all possess the thunder of pure fury and the calm breeze of tranquility. If it wasn't for tomorrow, how much would we get done today? Whatever your purpose . . . embrace it completely. Get lost in the clouds every now and then so you never lose sight of God's wonder.

—Paul Vitale

THE BIG QUESTIONS

If you go to your local bookstore and look for volumes on stress management, you'll find hundreds of titles. Most of them offer tips and techniques promising to lower tension and stress: breathing exercises, diet, sleep strategies, meditation, physical exercise, and on and on. Such strategies can be helpful, but they aren't the best place to start. We need to begin with the cosmic questions of meaning and purpose in life. If we get those right, we can then use the techniques to make progress. But if we get the answers to the big questions wrong (or completely ignore them as I did), all the techniques in the world will only rearrange the furniture on a sinking ship.

True success and peace of mind come from thinking deeply about—and finding the answers to—the questions that matter most:

- What is my source of security and significance?

- What matters to me more than anything else?

- What are my highest hopes and deepest fears?

- Who am I? Who do I want to become?

- Whose am I? To whom do I belong?

- What changes need to take place so that my life really counts?

You and I live in an age when only a rare minority of individuals desire to spend their lives in pursuit of objectives which are bigger than they are. In our age, for most people, when they die it will be as though they never lived.

—Rusty Rustenbach

Most people, even the most "successful" ones, are motivated to prove their value. They live with a nagging sense of insecurity, and they subconsciously strive to reach a point that declares, "I've made it! Look at me. I matter!" They work hard to climb the ladder, certain that each achieved goal will fill their hearts and give them the satisfaction they anticipated. And it does, but only for a few hours, or perhaps a few weeks. Then they realize they have to keep competing, keep jockeying, and keep winning to reach the next level . . . and the next . . . and the next.

True fulfillment, we realize sooner or later, doesn't come from our own accomplishments, but from investing in the lives of others. Who are the happiest people you know? Almost certainly, they're the ones who are pouring themselves into others as mentors, coaches, consultants, and friends. The success of others brings them life's greatest rewards.

Throughout my career, I've enjoyed meeting goals and reaching targets in my insurance business, speaking, and consulting, but I've realized the true value of those pursuits is that they give me the opportunity to give—financially, relationally, and in every other way—to help others reach their dreams. Giving thrills me more than anything else in my life.

The big questions force us to look beyond ourselves to find transcendent security and purpose. If we make our careers the source of our security and meaning, we'll be driven, and we'll use people as stepping-stones instead of valuing them as human beings. If we make our families the supreme source of our purpose in life, our moods will go up and down depending on the affirmation or criticism we're receiving from our spouse and kids. (One expert observed that parents are only as happy as their unhappiest child.) So we need a deeper, more permanent source of significance, one that fills the deep holes in our hearts so that we love people instead of using them, and we are motivated at work to contribute to the good of all instead of foolishly hoping the next big sale, commission, or promotion will finally give us the satisfaction we long for. Don't get me wrong. We can experience tremendous satisfaction at work, but only if success at work is a means to higher, deeper, more lasting purpose in our lives.

———————————— ❖ ————————————

The mystery of human existence lies not in just staying alive, but in finding something to live for.

—Fyodor Dostoyevsky

All of us need to find that transcendent source. I've found the ultimate security in the love, forgiveness, and acceptance of God through Jesus Christ, and I've found ultimate purpose because God has invited me to be His partner in having a profoundly positive impact on others. Ironically, this security and purpose doesn't dampen my drive, but rather redirects it. I can now pour all my energies into people, causes, and goals, but for a very different reason: not to *gain* security and significance, but because I *already have* security and significance.

Your search may lead you to the same source, or perhaps a different one. Ask the big questions, reach higher and dig deeper, and find a supreme source of security and purpose that gives meaning to every aspect of your life.

Many people are like I was for so many years. They're so focused on reaching financial and organizational goals they never even stop to ask the big questions. And nobody around them is asking, either. Everyone is laser-focused on the next rung up the ladder, the next big purchase, the next lavish vacation, or the next milestone that promises security and significance.

I wish I had stopped earlier to ask the big questions. I would have still had high goals, but I would have put them in a far bigger, broader, richer context of meaning and purpose. I would have enjoyed giving, supporting, and encouraging others earlier in my career. But I've also realized it's never too late to ask the right questions, uncover the right answers, and change the course of a life . . . even mine.

INESCAPABLE REALITIES

Let's be honest. There are no simple answers to the problems of stress in our lives. If we were hermits or monks or other people who had simple lives, the choices each day would be easy. But we live in an incredibly complex society. The demands for our attention seem infinite, but time is finite.

Complexity inevitably increases as we grow and take on additional responsibilities. Young singles may be able to balance work, friends, and leisure fairly effectively, but as they move up in an organization, the demands become more intense. When they get married, they don't have the option of communicating or not. And when they have kids, all bets are off! Having children changes our lives more than any other event, and three kids is twice as much work as two. The math doesn't sound right, but couples with three or more children can attest to this truth. Then sooner or later, those sweet, compliant children become teenagers! There's no need to explain how this fact can complicate life.

The answer isn't to neglect one major responsibility and focus on another—to forget about work, friends, and health to focus only on family, or any other configuration of a misguided single priority.

Some of us are gifted in one area, but very few are gifted in all of them. I'm good at business. I understand how it works, and I've been successful at it. But the rest of life is hard for me. Like most of us, I've gravitated toward my strength my entire life, while neglecting the other areas. Real happiness, I'm discovering, is finding the right balance, blending all elements in a beautiful mix of purpose, joy, tenacity, and love.

--- ❖ ---

To love what you do and feel that it matters—how could anything be more fun?

—Katherine Graham

It may surprise you to read this, but I don't believe stress is the real problem. The problem is too much *unrelieved* stress. A little stress uncorks our creative juices, revs our engines, and launches us to more meaningful interactions and greater accomplishments. All of us are different, so the capacity for stress varies, but all of us have a point at which too much stress, borne too long, begins to eat away our emotional, intellectual, volitional, and relational capacity.

In recent decades, pressures have multiplied in the lives of virtually every person in our culture. Only a couple of generations ago, most people worked for the same company their entire lives. Job security was taken for granted, but that's no longer the case. Today, most people are either looking over their shoulders to see if they're going to be fired, or they're looking for the door and the next opportunity.

A generation or two ago, people usually lived near their parents and grandparents. The family support system was intact and strong—but not today. The fabric of social relationships is torn so often by mobility that many people have no one near to depend on. The impact of these factors is both barely detectable and utterly devastating. Many of us live with such high levels of stress that it seems completely normal, yet constant stress effectively prevents a meaningful life of love, joy, and purpose. Existence becomes a grind, and it takes everything in us just to get up and go back into the fight every day.

Our stress has a direct impact on the people around us. When we're running on empty, we have nothing but fumes to offer them. I've talked to people who complain their spouses are driving them crazy because they are so stressed out. I want to say, "Friend, if you look in the mirror you'll see someone else who fits that description! Maybe your spouse is absorbing the toxicity you're pouring out when you get home each day." Subtle, huh? Still, it's necessary to look at the hard facts of stress, even if it takes someone else to point them out to us.

Finding meaning and balance isn't just a nice thing to do; it's not optional equipment on the vehicle of life. It's essential—for you, your family, your friends, and your colleagues. But none of us "gets it" immediately. We're creatures of habit, and our stress-filled patterns of life are long established and deeply entrenched. Changing them requires clear thinking, discipline, and finding new answers to the big questions in life. Change is a process, so I encourage you to be equally persistent and patient as you implement the concepts in this book.

----------------------- ❖ -----------------------

To serve is beautiful, but only if it is done with joy and a whole heart and a free mind.

—Pearl S. Buck

PULL OUT THE MAP

Some professions are fairly insular. For instance, people in the oil business often talk about colleagues who work in the "upstream" or "downstream" side of the industry, but they have little if any interaction with people outside the business. Similarly, people who work in finance spend most of their time around "numbers people." But those of us in the insurance business—as well as doctors, nurses, retail salespeople, attorneys, and some other careers—interact with people from all walks of life.

I regularly meet with people in all vocations and at every stage in their careers and families. In many cases I see their smiles reflect their genuine peace of mind. In their voices I hear stories of how their lives count. But I also see plenty of people whose faces and voices reflect the overwhelming pressure they endure each day. Some of them are so frazzled they see spending a few minutes with me as a hindrance, even though I'm trying to help them to the best of my ability. They feel too stressed to enjoy being served. Stress crushes, and it divides. It robs us of the things that make life worthwhile.

All of us are in the personal services business. You may be a dentist, or you may be the receptionist at the dentist's office. You may be the board chairman of a national trucking company, or you may be one of the drivers. You may work at a dress shop, or you may be a plumber. You may be a mid-level manager of a corporation, or you may be an intern. All of us, no matter what our calling may be, are profit centers for our companies. That term may sound cold, but it's not at all. We are effective employees only when we're at our best, managing our stress so that it stimulates us instead of eroding our creativity. And employers are most effective when they communicate their expectations clearly and often, enabling every person on the team to know how to bring value to the organization. Frankly, people at all levels of companies add stress to their lives by not understanding their roles and communicating expectations. Confusion ratchets up levels of stress.

I'm in the insurance and consulting business. I've written books and given seminars on all kinds of business-related topics, but this book is different from the others. This one is for the CEO and the person who makes deliveries, the front office and the field, those who consider themselves up-and-comers and those who feel like down-and-outers. All of us need to be honest enough to take a hard look at our lives, and we need the guts to make course changes when necessary.

—◆◆◆—

*That is happiness; to be dissolved into something completely
great.*

—Willa Cather

MY HOPE FOR YOU

As you read this book, I hope you learn the lessons I've been learning.
It's a process for me, and it will be a process for you—but by all means,
take courageous steps to redefine the big questions of your life so you find
more peace, meaning, and joy than you ever dreamed possible. When
you find that balance, you'll be able to be fully present with every person
you meet each day. You won't be constantly worried about your money,
and you won't be afraid of what others are thinking of you. You'll have
strength, stability, and security. Gradually, you'll become much more of
a giver than a taker, and you'll see the impact you're having on the people
who benefit from your expertise and care.

The principles in this book work for every faith tradition. I'm a
Christian, but the concepts I'm learning and sharing aren't limited in any
way. Whatever path you take, I hope your life becomes so full and meaningful that you touch countless others with the same peace and purpose
you find.

The path to peace is never smooth and easy. We experience resistance
from within and without. We naturally come up with excuses why we
can't change, how change will be too hard or too costly. And the people
around us may not feel comfortable with our forward progress. We might
assume they'll clap and shout for joy when we announce we're going to
reorient the most important priorities of our lives, but they may fight us
every step of the way.

No matter what, don't turn around. Keep reaching out and moving forward. Author and speaker John Ortberg encourages us to make the most of this pivotal point in our lives:

> The greatest moment of your life is now. Not because it's pleasant or happy or easy, but because this moment is the only moment you've got. Every past moment is irretrievably gone. It's never coming back. If you live there, you lose your life. And the future is always out there somewhere. You can spend an eternity waiting for tomorrow, or worrying about tomorrow. If you live there, you likewise will lose your life. This moment is God's irreplaceable gift to you.[3]

To make changes, you need three vital components: insight, direction, and courage. It's my goal to give you the first two, but it's up to you to provide the last one. I'll share insights and stories to give you fresh ideas about where your life can go, and I'll give you a roadmap to take steps in a new direction. The journey, though, won't happen without a large measure of tenacity as you keep taking steps on the road to a better, more balanced, and more fulfilling future.

At every stage of life—marriage, kids, promotion, college, kids' marriages, and all the rest—you'll have the challenge of reassessing what's important to you. Circumstances change, people change, and we change, so we need to reflect deeply and often about our direction. Don't be surprised, then, when old answers no longer seem to work as well as they did before. Dig deeper, find new answers, and keep moving forward.

Everyone—pantheist, atheist, skeptic, polytheist—has to answer these questions: "Where did I come from? What is life's meaning? How do I define right from wrong and what happens to me when I die?" Those are the fulcrum points of our existence.

—Ravi Zacharias

At the end of each chapter, you'll find some questions to help you think more deeply and apply the principles. The goal isn't to fill in the blanks, but instead, to consider the steps you can take to make your life more meaningful. If you're married, I encourage you to use these questions as discussion starters with your spouse. If you lead a team, use them to stimulate interaction and application. You'll get a lot more out of this book if you take a few minutes to reflect, and especially, if you talk about the content with others.

THINK ABOUT IT . . .

1. What about "balance," "peace," and "purpose" is most attractive to you?

2. Do any of those qualities seem unreachable? Explain your answer.

3. Look at the "big questions" again. How would you answer them today? Who can help you answer them more clearly?

4. What do you hope to get out of this book?

CHAPTER 2 | EMPTY PROMISES

Never forget that you are one of a kind. Never forget that if there weren't any need for you in all your uniqueness to be on this earth, you wouldn't be here in the first place. And never forget, no matter how overwhelming life's challenges and problems seem to be, that one person can make a difference in the world. In fact, it is always because of one person that all the changes that matter in the world come about. So be that one person.

—Richard Buckminster Fuller

Let me go back to the beginning and tell my story. When I started my career, I was given a "big book of business"—a phone book. The name of the strategy was "green field." It meant knocking on doors and making cold calls to see if people were interested in buying an insurance policy. Every encounter was a potential sale, so my manager encouraged me to see every conversation as a wide, fertile, green field ready for harvest.

However, after a year and a half of hard work, my field looked more like a desert. I struggled. In fact, I didn't sell the minimum number of life policies, so the company took away my subsidy guarantee program. In other words, I no longer got a check. I received a formal letter from the corporate office that said, "It's time for you to think about another career." It was the company's version of a Dear John letter. It screamed the one thing I dreaded to hear: "Troy, you're a failure!"

I was heartbroken. As I held the letter in my hands, my mind was flooded with memories of conversations when people had told me I shouldn't go into the insurance business—or any kind of sales. Suddenly I was faced with the hard fact that they might be right. In desperation and fear, I talked to Jay Green, my manager, and I tried to convince him I could do better. He was one of the most wonderful people I've ever known. At that critical moment in my life, Jay put his arm around my shoulders, looked me in the eye, smiled, and said, "Troy, here are the things you need to do to succeed in this business."

With a second chance, I was completely, utterly dedicated to success. My motivation, to be honest, wasn't just to serve my customers to the best of my ability. I was simply terrified to be labeled "a failure." Every morning I got out of bed thinking, *If I don't get enough leads, if I don't get enough appointments, if I don't give enough presentations, and I don't get enough sales, I'll be a loser, and I'll look like an idiot. I simply can't live with that!*

In my experience, there are two great motivators in life. One is fear. The other is love. You can manage an organization by fear, but if you do you will ensure that people won't perform up to their real capabilities.

—Jan Carlson, Chairman and CEO of Scandinavian Airlines

In that season of my life, I read voraciously. I read books and listened to tapes on sales and marketing, psychology, business, and successful people. A common principle described in these books and messages is that fear is the most toxic form of motivation. A certain kind of fear—the response to immediate danger—is good and right and helpful because it propels us to take action to protect others and ourselves. A threat occurs, we respond, and it's over. But that's not the kind of fear I was experiencing. I lived under the constant, nagging weight of dread and impending doom, wondering if I could make it and afraid there would be no open doors for the rest of my life if I didn't. This kind of fear doesn't produce anything good, noble, and right. It kills, and it almost killed me.

Part of the problem during my first seven years in business was that I felt terribly alone. My manager was very positive and encouraging, but I always knew I had to perform . . . or else. Then one day I went to see my dentist for a cleaning and checkup. The appointment changed my life. When I walked in, the receptionist greeted me warmly and said it would only be a few minutes before the hygienist would come to get me. Next to the receptionist, I noticed someone answering the phone and making calls to confirm appointments. In a small office off the waiting area, I saw someone replacing files for patients they'd just seen and taking out files for new appointments. When the hygienist took me back, I noticed how seamlessly she and the dentist worked together.

My observations that day may not have seemed significant to anyone else, but they were revolutionary for me. In my office, I didn't have anyone other than myself to greet my customers, and I was often preoccupied doing something else when they walked in. I didn't have anyone fielding calls and confirming appointments. I had to be on the phone for hours each day to make sure my schedule stayed full. I spent many more hours each week doing my own filing and paperwork. I didn't have an associate to work alongside me to serve our customers.

Like an existential game of dodge ball, I had been on the defense, outnumbered and overpowered, trying desperately to keep from being floored by any of the endless barrage of balls thrown at me all day every day. I had been a one-man show, but I was determined not to be alone any longer. I began to recruit and select members of a team. One of the first was someone to perform the functions I'd seen in the dentist's office—I called this person my Agency Contact Representative. When I had my ACR, I could finally go on the offensive to control my schedule and be far more productive. As my new team began to hum, my stress levels went way down and my peace of mind soared. My income level rose, too.

For a while I thought I had it made, but I soon realized that hiring the right people and putting them in the right places is an enormous challenge. I made plenty of mistakes, and each blunder multiplied my stress again. With a team, I had more opportunities for success and growth, but I also had far more loose ends (primarily relationships in the office) to manage every day. Over the years, I've hired some wonderful, gifted, dedicated people, but I've also hired some who had little competency, dedication, or relational skills. Dumb decisions. Really dumb decisions.

As I attended to difficulties on my team, I wondered if the dentist had as much trouble hiring the right people as I did. Managing my team became a full-time job: interviewing, hiring, onboarding, training, supervising, and dealing with the inevitable failures and conflicts. My stress level was right back where it had been before, and in some ways it was even worse. Now I was afraid to fail because our agency was much bigger, so the fallout would gouge a larger and more devastating impact crater if we failed.

Doing more things faster is no substitute for doing the right things.

—**Stephen Covey**

The solution to my first season of stress was to put a team together. The solution to the second season was to construct a system for our team, a *repeatable process* that produced predictable order, consistency, and stability in our operations.

Frankly, I depended on stability in our office because I needed a safe place where I knew what was going to happen each day. I often felt tremendous stress at home because of health concerns for our children and the tension this always creates. In addition, I often experienced stress in other relationships with friends and acquaintances. With a system in place at work, I could escape chaos and have eight to ten hours of order, predictability, and peace every day. I wanted to create an environment in our office that worked like a charm, one that relieved my stress instead of increasing it.

For years, the system worked incredibly well. Our business grew, and leaders asked me for advice. After a while, I realized I could create new roles as a platform speaker and a consultant. I suddenly had income streams from several lucrative sources. Money hides a lot of problems, but it can also make a person stupid. I started investing in companies outside my expertise. A few of them did well, but I wasted a ton of money on those that failed. When I look back on all those awful decisions, I realize I thought every one of them looked brilliant before I wrote the check. It doesn't take much detailed analysis to see one of the biggest problems during this period: every bad decision was in some way related to alcohol. Drinking made me feel invincible, but it actually made me foolish.

Success sometimes carries the seeds of its own destruction. I began to spend money like crazy, and I encouraged family, friends, and business partners to depend on me far too much. I was enabling many of them financially. It made me feel like a hero, but it wasn't good for them.

For most of my career, the theme of my life was "growin' and goin.'" My adopted theme song was by Tom Petty:

It's time to move on, time to get going
What lies ahead, I have no way of knowing
But under my feet, baby, grass is growing
It's time to move on, it's time to get going.[4]

No matter what happened, I just kept moving forward. Relationships shattered, but I kept going. Some of my investments tanked, but I looked for the next one. Friendships split up, so I gravitated toward new ones. My personal life was falling apart, but I was successful in my business. Companies paid me a lot of money to give lectures to their people. My books, especially *Power Position Your Agency*, were widely read and became required in courses at several universities. In my agency, in lecturing and consulting, and in my other ventures, I lived for the thrill of the chase. The adrenaline rush of winning in business gave me an identity and the energy to keep moving. If I'd looked behind me, I would have seen signs of significant devastation in the wake of my speedboat, but I seldom looked back.

I didn't understand it then, but now I realize much of my drive was a desperate need to control everyone and everything around me. At the first crisis point in my career, I had been motivated by the dark, foreboding fear of failure, but the fear hadn't gone away as I climbed the ladder of success. At every new stage of success, I found more people to control and better systems to control them. I had to have all the answers for my customers and my staff. When any decision needed to be made, I had to make it. I made sure that all inquiries found their way to my office, but I was overwhelmed. In fact, the stacks of files on my desk got so high that I began putting stacks on the floor so no one would see them. I wasn't merely collecting all those papers; I was hoarding them!

I simply couldn't keep up with the multiplying volume of information and decisions. Quite often, customers called to get a quote or an answer to a question, but I was busy dealing with a thousand other points of minutia. Each time, my failure to come through doubled my anxiety and my fear of failure.

At each stage of growth, I expected my fear to subside. It didn't. My coping strategies just became more sophisticated, and my fear became better hidden and more seductive—and it was masked by a much larger income. Success had promised to fill the hole in my soul, but it was an empty promise. No amount of success—even fulfilling my wildest dreams of acclaim, power, and financial security—could bring the kind of security and peace I longed for.

Many men go fishing all of their lives without knowing it is not fish they are after.

—Henry David Thoreau

OVER THE LIMIT

As I've said, experiences of mild to moderate stress can activate creativity. However, when we're in prolonged seasons of unrelenting tension, the pressure often rises so gradually that we don't even notice, so we fail to make necessary adjustments. Under this pressure, our reserves are used up, our abilities decline, and we make an inordinate number of bad decisions. Also, our emotions are affected: we feel anger and resentment (often without being able to identify the target of our anger), we suffer physical symptoms like headaches and stomach problems, our relationships struggle because we're grumpy, and we're less effective in everything we do. At that point, we can experience the devastation of burnout.[5]

The stress experienced by some people in business, the nonprofit world, and churches can be compared to combat fatigue or compassion fatigue. Officers in the Civil War noticed that the effectiveness of many soldiers was diminished by the strain of battle. Thousands had to be taken out of battle lines to recuperate, but doctors and generals understood very little about this problem. About fifty years later during World War I, intense artillery bombardments caused hundreds of thousands of soldiers to become emotionally and psychologically devastated—a condition physicians labeled "shell shock." In World War II, officers and doctors finally grasped the impact of continuous combat. They noticed that the effectiveness of soldiers sharply deteriorated if they were in battle more than ninety days during the course of the war. In "Combat Exhaustion," a study by Army psychiatrists, research showed that a soldier "became steadily less valuable [after ninety days in action] until he was completely useless."[6] The PBS documentary, *The Perilous Fight*, reported on American soldiers in the Pacific theater: An astounding "1,393,000 soldiers were treated for battle fatigue during World War II. Of all ground combat troops, 37 percent were discharged for psychiatric reasons."[7]

Soldiers returning from Iraq and Afghanistan suffer at an alarming rate from Post-Traumatic Stress Syndrome (PTSD), while others in our communities suffer from what some have titled "compassion fatigue," a mild form of PTSD commonly associated with doctors, nurses, pastors, chaplains, and charity workers. The condition can also be associated with tenderhearted, kind people who haven't established adequate boundaries, limitations, and self-care while helping sick and needy people.

An article in *The Online Journal of Issues in Nursing* explains the nature of compassion fatigue:

[Compassion fatigue (CF)] symptomology is nearly identical to that of post traumatic stress disorder (PTSD), except CF applies to caregivers who were affected by the trauma of others. Caregivers with CF may develop a preoccupation with their patients by re-experiencing their trauma; they can develop signs of persistent arousal and anxiety as a result of this secondary trauma. Examples of this arousal can include difficulty falling or staying asleep, irritability or outbursts of anger, and/or exaggerated startle responses. Most importantly, these caregivers ultimately experience a reduced capacity for, or interest in being empathic toward the suffering of others.

The article goes on to detail other specifics of compassion fatigue, and then concludes with this observation:

The impact of CF can extend beyond paid (formal) healthcare providers. Symptoms of CF have been recognized in informal caregivers, such as family members who care for loved ones who have been directly traumatized by past experiences. These caregivers can experience CF symptoms as they become preoccupied by their relative's condition. This may result in irritability with frequent outbursts of anger and a reduced capacity for caregiving. The health of these caregivers must not be ignored, especially since the value of the care they provide is very high.[8]

In addition to these identifiable causes and effects, we might label the impact of prolonged, unrelieved stress in a business context as "competition fatigue." The symptoms are much like the others: being obsessed with responsibilities, outbursts of anger, a negative outlook, and a lower standard of performance, even though it seems like the person is trying harder than ever.

If this kind of fatigue isn't identified and addressed, the person is at risk of suffering an emotional, relational, and vocational collapse. Before this happens, it's time to get help. When the oxygen masks drop during an emergency on a plane flight, you're told to first secure your own source of oxygen and then help others with you. The same principle is true for those who are gasping for air at work and at home. If *you're* a wreck, you won't be much help to anyone else.

Sadly, we sometimes give everything we've got at work and have almost nothing left when we walk through the door at home. We wish we could be engaged in family conversations and enjoy activities with our spouse and children, but we're either too late or too exhausted. Then we realize we've failed at our most fundamental commitments, and we feel intense guilt on top of all the other stress we're carrying. Little disagreements erupt in explosions, easily resolved problems become nightmares, and the people we love the most become our biggest threats. If we suffer this kind of discord under our own roofs, we may feel more confident and comfortable giving ourselves to those outside our families, people who don't know us as well and can't hurt us if we disappoint them. To compound the problem, we may hold the people closest to us to an unreasonably high standard, expecting them to be deeply appreciative of our efforts and never disappoint us—which, of course, inevitably leads to deep disappointment, hurt, and division. It's a vicious cycle.

THE "DISNEY" LIFE

If asked to name a place where dreams come true, many people think of Disneyland, which is called "The Happiest Place on Earth!" Actually, Walt Disney's creations were largely a reaction to rampant unhappiness. He grew up in a very poor family, and he often felt like an outsider in the schools he attended. Because he felt he had been denied a happy childhood, he wanted to create a place where other children could be supremely happy. Deep discouragement was the fuel that produced incredible creativity and an atmosphere of delight. Unfortunately for Walt Disney, he was so driven that he seldom enjoyed the sheer pleasure he was creating for others. Still, Disneyland has produced the ultimate expectation of happiness for millions of people in America and around the world. I love learning about brilliant, bold, creative, complex people— Walt Disney was certainly one of those at the top of the list.[9]

But we dare not confuse Disneyland with the real world. A friend told me that he knows a young woman who lives on a roller coaster of emotions because she always hopes her life will be as wonderful as Disneyland, but when reality proves to be something short of ideal, she feels deeply hurt and betrayed. We might laugh and say this young woman's perceptions are ridiculous, but studies show that to some degree advertising has a similar impact on virtually all of us.

The goal of advertising isn't merely to present the attributes of toothpaste, cereal, or banking. The goal is to create dissatisfaction in potential consumers, a perception that we simply can't be happy, fulfilled, and popular unless we buy this product or use that service. In the early years of television, French cultural philosopher Jacque Ellul observed that the goal of advertising is to create needs, not to meet them. He remarked, "When men [and women] feel and respond to the needs advertising creates, they are adhering to its ideal of life. The human tendencies upon which advertising like this is based may be strikingly simpleminded, but they nonetheless represent pretty much the level of our modern life. Advertising offers us the ideal we have always wanted."[10]

Ellul wrote during the era of Madison Avenue shown on the series *Mad Men*. What would he say about today's far more advanced marketing machine? We're not talking about illegal manipulation of the facts about a product to purposely deceive people. Instead, modern ads present their products in a way that promises to open the doors to love, security, and excitement. For instance, a soft drink may temporarily quench your thirst, but the ad shows young, fit, happy people enjoying the beverage and having the time of their lives. The not-so-subtle message is that the colored water in the bottle will give each of us the same wonderful, warm relationships we crave. It's a seductive message, and to some degree, we soak it in without critical analysis . . . so we believe it.

One factor that increases stress and disappointment for many people is unrealistic expectations. Largely due to advertising, women today compare their appearance with the most gorgeous models in the world, the airbrushed beauties who grace the pages of fashion magazines and the designers' catwalks. If normal women feel they have to compete with supermodels, it's no wonder they feel inferior. And men compare their abs, their cars, their bank accounts, and their clothes to the sexiest, richest images money can buy in the advertising world. Anyone who tries to compete always feels second-class, longing for more and willing to buy the next overhyped product.

Real stress, combined with unrealistic expectations, multiplies pressure, heartache, and despair.

Understanding the difference between healthy striving and perfectionism is critical to laying down the shield and picking up your life. Research shows that perfectionism hampers success. In fact, it's often the path to depression, anxiety, addiction, and life paralysis.

—Brené Brown

TRYING TO COPE

When the tension gets too high, we look for a way to relieve it. Too often, though, we look for a quick and easy way to relieve the *effects* of the pressure we feel, not a way that actually addresses the *cause* of the problem. I know; I think I've tried them all. Let me identify just a few common coping strategies:

- *Double down*—In the early stages of stress, most of us have a simple solution: we strive harder to try to catch up, please the boss or clients, and make things work. Of course, if the cause of our stress is that we've been irresponsible, working harder is exactly the right solution. But for most of us, adding hours to the workday, days to the workweek, and files to our desks isn't a workable long-term solution. This strategy increases stress and makes a crash inevitable.

- *Eliminate and focus*—The squeaky wheel gets the grease, so whoever is barking at us gets our attention. If a particular client is demanding increased efforts, we forget everything else and work hard to please him. If a spouse or child complains that we aren't attentive, we drop everything to be there. Some of us live a "whack-a-mole" life, jumping from one insistent need to another, but not even noticing that others need us, too. In this attempt, we've given up on any semblance of balance, wisdom, and peace.

- *Distractions*—Some people go in a very different direction to relieve stress. Instead of being more focused, they become less attentive to the problem. In fact, they don't even want to think about it! If they ignore it, they assume, it won't bother them. They go on social media sites, play videogames, read, watch sports, or do anything to take their minds off of the demands of work and home.

- **Blame others**—When things go wrong, some of us instinctively point fingers at anybody and everybody else. We don't want to take the heat, so we go through all kinds of linguistic gymnastics to convince others that we aren't to blame. We may overtly tell others "It was her fault!" or we may use less direct methods of gossip and innuendo.

- **Numbing**—Alcohol, illegal drugs, and the misuse of prescription drugs can deaden heartache, anger, and hurt for a while, but when the chemicals wear off, they leave the person even more ashamed and desperate to use again. Addictive behaviors like gambling, shopping, hoarding, and illicit sex trigger self-made brain chemicals to mask the pain and emptiness of life and provide a short-term buzz. In a *Boston Globe* article, Jonah Lehrer noted the change in brain chemistry among those who are compulsive gamblers: "From the perspective of the brain, gambling has much in common with addictive drugs, like cocaine. Both work by hijacking the brain's pleasure centers—a lure that some people are literally incapable of resisting."[11]

- **Drop out**—Escape can take many forms. A person may legitimately realize she's in the wrong role and request a transfer, or she may crack under the pressure and never come back to the office. Some have to take a few days off, even in the middle of a busy schedule, because they've hit the wall of exhaustion. The ultimate dropout is suicide, a desperate option taken by far too many people who have lost all hope of finding a solution to their pain and loneliness.

Under too much stress, we lose the sense of purpose that thrills our souls and inspires us to greatness, leaving only the desperate hope to make it through one more day. Our goal then is only to survive. We're made for more than that . . . much more.

TOO MUCH TOO OFTEN

I've seen people in all walks of life who have cratered under relentless pressure. We call it burnout. They withstood the stresses of home, business, health, and finances as long as they could, but eventually, like a branch that is bent to the breaking point, they snapped. Finding a remedy earlier would have required significant changes to refocus, regroup, and recoup energies, but the remedy *after* burnout requires far, far more time, attention, professional care, and healing.

Frederick was a star outfielder on his high school baseball team, and he earned a full scholarship to play for a major college team. There, he continued to excel, earning all-conference honors his last two years. He was a bright young man who earned a degree in accounting and then an MBA. A number of major accounting firms wanted him to join them. Not long after he started his promising career, he married a beautiful girl. They were the picture of a young, successful couple.

Within a few years, Frederick was flourishing as a CPA. He and his wife had two children, and they lived in a fine home in one of the best neighborhoods in the city. Gradually, the pressures of being the person who made major decisions every day for wealthy individuals and corporations began to take their toll. Frederick became irritated at small problems with his staff. His growing kids needed more of his time, but he gave them less. His wife's reasonable requests sounded like incessant nagging. An unmarried colleague noticed the rising stress in Frederick's life, so he advised him to blow off some steam by joining him for a card game after work. The drinking, gambling, and laughing were a relief, so Frederick began joining the game several nights a week. The drinking numbed the pain of his stressful life, so Frederick began to drink even more.

Frederick's wife saw what was happening to him, but her pleas for sobriety and responsibility only incited Frederick to outbursts of anger. Over the next two years, they lived in an armed truce. Occasionally she yelled at him, then wept and walked out of the house for a few hours, but nothing changed.

Finally, his wife had had enough. She threatened to get a divorce, and the kids, barely old enough to know what was going on, were confused and scared by the anger between their mom and dad. Quiet rumors about Frederick quickly spread into common knowledge in the community. A respected accountant—and his whole family—now lived in disgrace. Who would go to him now for financial advice? And his wife didn't know who among her friends would remain close . . . and who would drop her like a hot rock.

When the full reality of his foolish choices hit him, Frederick asked to meet with me. The strong, confident athlete and professional had become a beaten man with hollow eyes. He wept and wondered aloud, "How in the world could I have let this happen? And what am I going to do now? I know what I am, but I don't have the tools to dig myself out of this hole."

The chief cause of failure and unhappiness is trading what we want most for what we want now.

—Zig Ziglar

Sarah was a woman who arrived at the same place of despair, but through a different route. She and her husband had four children, but her husband was emotionally distant from her and the kids. She tried her best to look pretty and cook his favorite foods, but nothing attracted his attention. One day she noticed a message on his phone from someone confirming an appointment. She tried to ignore it, but within a few weeks, her curiosity prompted her to check his phone several times when he wasn't looking. She returned one of the calls and discovered the "appointment" was with a prostitute. When she angrily confronted him, he, of course, denied her allegation. Distrust and acrimony quickly escalated, and her husband moved out. She filed for a divorce, but the damage wasn't over after it was final.

Sarah poured her affection into her children. She was determined to make up for their father's lack of love for them. She smothered them with attention, even when they were teenagers and needed to carve out their own identity. Just after the divorce, she got a job selling ads for a local newspaper. She was good at it, but her heart was always with her children. The more attention she gave them, the more they pulled away. Their resistance broke her heart. But it was more than resistance: her children, the focus of her existence, despised her for not respecting their ability to make at least some of their own decisions. In their unveiled fury, they blamed her for the failed marriage. Sarah thought all she was doing for them was pure love, but actually, she was desperately craving their love to heal the gaping wound in her own heart. Of course, she couldn't see this insight at the time.

The pain of a failed marriage, and now estranged children, was too much for Sarah. She got a prescription for pain, a pain she made up when she saw her doctor, and she began abusing the painkillers. At work she smiled and tried to act like she was on top of the world, but her foggy mind affected her performance. Her managing editor tried to talk to her about her personal life, but for Sarah, the chaos at home and in her heart was too painful to share. Within months, she spiraled down into self-hatred, depression, and isolation. Eventually she lost her job after failing yet again to make an appointment with a client. At that point, she had nothing . . . literally nothing.

I have a number of clients in the trucking industry. I was impressed with Charles, a driver for one of the big freight lines, due to his intelligence and appearance—he was a very handsome man. He told me he made more than $150,000 a year, but he was currently living in the extended cab of his truck. He drank, but seldom to excess. He tried investing in a local company, but it went under. He had been married, but his wife left him. He had three grown children, but he rarely talked to them.

Charles took a deep breath and continued his story. On the outside, he looked like a very normal, likeable guy, but he had a secret: he gambles, and he gambles a lot. Years earlier, he began playing poker with some friends, but soon he found a game with men who were serious about cards. For Charles, poker became an obsession. He won enough to give him momentary thrills, but within a year, he blew tens of thousands of dollars. He hid his losses from his wife as long as he could.

To cover his losses, Charles made large bets, but his losing streak didn't end. Only months later, he found himself so far in debt that he borrowed money from friends. Lying became a way of life, and he was so preoccupied with his debts that his career suffered. When strange men showed up at the door one day demanding payment, his wife panicked. Finally the truth came out, and his wife felt betrayed. After a few months of promises and lies, she took the children and left him.

When I talked to him, Charles was a shattered man. Gambling had destroyed his self-confidence and ruined his most important relationships. As he told me about his plight, it was obvious his obsession and his secret had torpedoed him. After about an hour of talking together, he shook his head and tried to laugh, but then a tear trickled down his face. He told me, "Troy, I don't know what in the world happened to me. I've made such a disaster of my life."

Some people assume having plenty of money is the answer to all of life's problems. It's not. I know a woman who was so poor in the 1950s that she had to make a living as an orderly serving meals and changing sheets in a hospital. After work, she went to a bar to get a drink. She met the owner, and soon they fell in love and got married. Her husband proved to be a shrewd businessman. He bought an entire block of the downtown of a sleepy little village on the ocean in Florida. He opened several businesses, and he hit the jackpot: in a few years the population boomed, and the little town became one of the hottest properties in the state. His land and buildings were now worth tens of millions of dollars. The woman and her husband were fabulously rich, but somehow, she couldn't enjoy her prosperity. She still shopped at second-hand stores, bought day-old bread and clipped coupons. She continued to live like the woman changing sheets for a living, even though she could have bought the hospital!

Unfortunately, I know a lot of other men and women who have suffered the devastation of burnout and personal destruction. The situations are widely varied, but these people almost always experience the cascading effects of multiple stresses. All of them, though, have one thing in common: they didn't pay attention to the warning signs.

WARNING SIGNS

I tried for many years to ignore the warning signs in my own life. I have a high threshold of pain, so my solution to every struggle in life has been to tell myself, "Come on, Troy! Get over it! Suck it up and keep going!" This strategy worked for thirty years in business, but the well of self-motivation and determination eventually ran dry. One day I looked in the mirror and had to admit I was clinically depressed. I needed more help than pumping myself up one more time. I had worked myself to the bone, but I didn't feel appreciated. I tried to help a friend, but he stole money from me. I invested in promising business ventures that bombed. I hired people I was sure would be great on our team, but some of them were self-serving and poisoned the atmosphere of our office. Many things that had turned to gold so often before now were turning to dust.

Self-justification no longer was enough to make me feel better, and venting my emotions to anyone who would listen wasn't good for them or me. I had to find a different way, a healthier way, a more productive way to heal the pain and discover a renewed sense of purpose. And I needed to find a friend who could help me take the necessary steps.

Some people suffer from a traumatic event that changes their lives forever. They have no problem pointing to the cause of their heartache. But for most of us, the gradual rise in our level of stress is more like the proverbial frog in the kettle. One minute, we're swimming comfortably, and we hardly notice that the water is getting a little hotter over time. But after a while, we're boiled!

Let me give you a checklist of signs and symptoms of a person whose water is getting too hot:

- **Emotional signs**

    Moody
    Explosions of anger
    Unspecified anxiety
    Feeling alone
    Prolonged disappointment and discouragement

- **Relational signs**

    Blaming others when you're responsible
    Willing to accept blame even when it wasn't your fault
    Avoiding friends and family

Depending too much on friends and family

Trusting untrustworthy people or not trusting anyone

- *Cognitive signs*

   Obsessive thoughts

   Assuming the worst is going to happen

   Impulsive decisions

   Poor concentration

   Forgetfulness

- *Behavioral signs*

   Eating too much or too little

   Sleeping too much or too little

   Neglecting responsibilities

   Using chemicals to numb the pain or unwise behaviors to
      escape

   Isolating

   Unwilling to take risks

   Loss of confidence

- *Physical signs*

   Stomach ailments, nausea, constipation, diarrhea

   Frequent headaches

   Rapid heartbeat

   Exhaustion, even with adequate sleep

   Loss of sex drive

I consider myself somewhat of an expert on stress—not because I'm a clinician or have mastered the art of living well, but because I've made so many mistakes and had so many opportunities to learn crucial lessons. I sometimes tell people that I've written four books that are bestsellers in the insurance industry, but I could have easily written twenty books on the stupid things I've done in my life and my career.

WAKE UP!

As you've read this chapter, you've undoubtedly conducted a silent inventory of the stress in your life and your reactions to it. One of the things we need to realize is that even the good things in life—graduation, marriage, having children, vacations, promotions, and other victories—also add to our stress because they create change. The collection of stressors, pleasant and painful, can add up and push a person beyond the breaking point.

I encourage you to notice the heat of the water you're in right now. Is it hotter than it was a few months ago? If so, are you doing anything to reduce the temperature, or will you ignore it until you're boiled? To use a different metaphor, is the level of your emotional tank rising or falling? Are you regularly feeding your soul with faith, friends, laughter, and relaxation? Or are you using destructive, short-term coping techniques just to make it through one more day?

The stages of burnout are alarm, resistance, and exhaustion. Pay attention to the alarm bells, and don't resist the messages from your body, your attitude, and those who love you. Don't let shame keep you a prisoner. The longer you minimize the problem, make excuses, and deny the hard realities of unrelieved tension, the more you keep sliding toward the devastation of burnout.

It may or may not be much consolation, but at least you can know you're not alone. A lot of people are trying really hard to make life work, yet keep falling behind. A Jackson Browne song describes many of us:

Looking out at the road rushing under my wheels
I don't know how to tell you all just how crazy this life feels
I look around for the friends I used to turn to, to pull me through
Looking into their eyes I see them running too
Running on, running on empty
Running on, running blind
Running on, running into the sun, but I'm running behind.[12]

Don't let these lyrics describe you any longer. Get the help you need. You may need to see a doctor, a therapist, a nutritionist, or a pastor . . . or maybe all of them. But don't put it off. Your life, your most treasured relationships, and your sanity depend on your taking action.

The good news is that no one is beyond repair. We may have done considerable damage to our bodies, our relationships, and our minds by not paying attention to the warning signs, but we can start now. The road back to sanity, security, and significance starts with the first glimpse of honesty.

Losers live in the past. Winners learn from the past and enjoy working in the present toward the future.

—Dennis Waitley

THINK ABOUT IT . . .

1. How would you compare and contrast combat fatigue, compassion fatigue, and competition fatigue?

2. How do the promises of advertising add to your sense of disappointment and stress? What are your favorite commercials? What are the seductive promises in each one?

3. To some degree, all of us use coping mechanisms to manage stress. Which one(s) do you use most often? Why does it work? How does it actually harm you?

4. Where are you in the stages of alarm, resistance, and exhaustion?

5. Do you need to get help? Why or why not? What is your next (or first) step? Who can help you?

CHAPTER 3 | **PIPEDREAM?**

The two most important days of your life are the day you are born and the day you find out why.

—Mark Twain

Is it really possible to have a balanced life? Can we figure out how to live with real peace and a thrilling purpose?

Our goal isn't to create a life completely free from concerns. That'll never happen. If we love people, we'll be concerned when they inevitably struggle. When we have goals, we'll be disappointed when we don't meet them. Life has plenty of ups and downs for even the most balanced, mature, sane, and secure people. The questions, then, are: Can we experience a peace so deep that the pressures of life can't obliterate it, and can we find a purpose so compelling that setbacks don't erode it? Or is this kind of peace and purpose just words on a page . . . a pipedream?

HONESTY AND ACTION

The first step in making a change is to be ruthlessly objective about where we are. If we're hiking, we can't get to a destination on a map without first knowing where we're standing. The trail may lead up or down, left or right, backward or forward, so first we need to know the truth about our current position.

But pinpointing our current position doesn't take us to our destination, and objectivity alone doesn't produce real, lasting change. We then have to take action, and keep taking action over time so that we make genuine progress. Hiking is a perfect metaphor for life. When we hike in the mountains, we can get lost and have to turn around to find the trail again. Or we may climb for hours and think we're close to the top, only to realize we've been looking at a false peak a thousand feet below the summit. The path may be easy or hard, but it's a path that requires us to keep walking, keep taking action, and keep moving toward our goal.

In my near burnout condition, I had to be more honest than ever before—about my situation, my relationships, and the patterns of thinking and acting that led me into the blind canyon of deep despair. I took stock of how I'd tried to cope—by numbing the pain, using anger to intimidate and control people, and never really relaxing. I had to admit that I wasn't even doing the simplest things to be physically and emotionally healthy. When I'm depressed, I stop exercising, which then stops the flow of endorphins that provides energy and hope. And when I'm depressed, I isolate myself from people who love and encourage me. In my despair, I assume they don't want to be with me, or I'll ruin their day with my sour mood. I don't even give them the chance to speak truth, life, and peace into my life.

An accurate analysis of the destructive behaviors makes identifying the positive ones intuitively obvious. Immediately, I realized I needed to take daily walks whether I felt motivated to go or not, and I began spending time with people who understand me and love me so they could fill my emotional tank.

I realized, too, that not everyone who is available can fill this vital role. My tendency is to just find a listening ear and spill my guts. It gradually dawned on me that this strategy wasn't helpful to me or to most of the people I talked to. Some of them couldn't grasp the complexity of my situation, so they gave me simplistic solutions when all I wanted them to do was to listen. We don't need a dozen true friends, but we desperately need one or two. We need people who have the capacity to know us intimately without feeling compelled to fix us, and who love us enough to genuinely care. If we sense someone loves us without truly knowing us, the love seems superficial. Or if the person knows everything about us but doesn't love us, we feel vulnerable, exposed, and terrified. Knowing and loving—both are essential in a true friend.

Another action step I had to take, and continue to take often, was to choose gratitude. That may sound strange for a person who has been so abundantly blessed, but depression has a way of putting blinders on our eyes so we don't even see the many blessings of life. I took time to think about my mother. I've never met a more wonderful human being; she is incredibly wise and supportive. As a single mom, she did a superb job of raising her kids. As I thought about her (and think about her now), my heart is filled with wonder and gratitude. I know many families in which the siblings barely tolerate each other, but I have terrific relationships with mine.

You cannot change your destination overnight, but you can change your direction overnight.

—Jim Rohn

My sister Sharon is my business partner. She runs our insurance agency, and I trust her implicitly. My older brother Alan works with me with me in my consulting business. My brother Keith runs our restaurant called

Crawdaddy's in Visalia. He's a fabulous musician and a talented restaurateur. It's a tough business, but he has made it a powerhouse of dining and entertainment. My sister Stacy, Sharon's twin, owns a thriving insurance agency on the central coast of California. Stacy is consistently one of the top agents in the country, and we swap insights and ideas all the time. My wife and children love me. I have the greatest kids in the world. I couldn't have a more wonderful support system than my family. During the time in my life when I felt deep despair, I took them for granted, or maybe I just overlooked their love and kindness. For me, progress meant refocusing my mind on the enormous blessing these dear people are to me.

I also needed to make better choices about the people with whom I hung around. I've always gravitated toward people, but I had begun to lean toward those who were living on the edge, people who seemed to go for broke in everything they do. They were more exciting that those who were full of peace and cautious wisdom, but their influence on me wasn't positive. Almost three thousand years ago, King Solomon observed, "Walk with the wise and become wise; associate with fools and get in trouble" (Prov. 13:20). Similarly, Zig Ziglar commented, "Some people brighten a room by entering it; others when they leave. Attitudes are contagious." If the big risk-takers in my life didn't leave the room, I needed to leave it. My room needed to become brighter one way or another.

I live in the greatest country in the world. Sure, we can gripe about politics or the weather or taxes or a hundred other things, but I had to make a determined effort to stop focusing on the negative. Instead, I determined to rivet my mind on all the positives. There are plenty of people throwing stones, especially if you're in the public eye in any way, but I have a loving, wise, supportive network of family and friends I can count on. As I thought about them, I realized I could call them at any time of the day or night and ask for help, and every one of them would instantly drop what they were doing and come to help me. I can count on them through thick and thin. I had forgotten that fact.

It's a dictum of life to worry only about the things you can directly control, but I'd neglected this basic truth. My mind had become consumed with all the "should haves" of the past and the "what ifs" of the future. I wasn't enjoying each moment God had given me because I was fretting so much about things that were beyond my control. To correct this problem, I began the hard work of figuring out what I'm actually responsible to be and do. This isn't an easy task for a person who has been hyper-responsible and overcommitted, but it's necessary.

I had gotten into trouble by depending only on my own wits, and I realized I needed to find experts who could help me progress on my journey to peace and purpose. Physicians, counselors, nutritionists, and pastors can provide a booster shot of wisdom and hope, but that may not be enough. I also needed to find at least one person to hold me accountable. Quite often, this person is a therapist or a close friend. It doesn't really matter who it is, as long as we find someone who is willing to ask us the hard questions—especially when we don't want to answer them. I don't need someone who is intimidated by my success or my demeanor. I need someone who can look beneath my crusty exterior and see the hurting person who wants to escape the pain more than have it slowly healed. I need someone who loves me enough to speak the truth to me even when I don't want to listen.

Character cannot be developed in ease and quiet. Only through experience of trial and suffering can the soul be strengthened, ambition inspired, and success achieved.

—Helen Keller

SECOND CHANCES

We love to hear—and we need to hear—stories about people who failed miserably but took advantage of second chances. It appeared that Martha Stewart's career would end when she was sent to prison, but she came back as an icon of food and fashion. Robert Downey, Jr. seemed to throw his life away on drugs, but he has made a remarkable turn in his career. In sports, film, politics, business, and every other walk of life, we can find men and women who appeared to be completely and utterly done, but who took advantage of second chance opportunities.

We don't have to read the newspapers to find courageous people who turned hopelessness into hope. Every meeting of Alcoholics Anonymous and other recovery groups is filled with people who have made dramatic changes or are in the process of making them. I have the greatest respect for these men and women. Because their attendance is anonymous, we may not realize they live next door, down the street, or sit next to us in synagogue or church each week. This kind of authenticity and bravery can be found in a wide variety of people who endure struggles. Let me tell you about a few people whose courage makes them heroes.

Antidote

Chad is a good friend and a client. His father was a successful businessman, so Chad had many advantages when he was growing up. After graduating from college and getting an MBA, he joined one of the large investment companies. He married a beautiful woman, and they had two kids. Everything he touched, it seemed, was pure gold. His future looked very bright.

Fundraisers wanted Chad to attend events because they knew he'd attract a crowd, and everyone throwing a party wanted him, too. He was magnetic, the kind of person everyone wants to be with. He enjoyed the social life, and he often stayed at parties long after his wife went home.

He enjoyed having drinks with his friends, not only at parties, but every afternoon after work at the bar around the corner from his office. But each morning, he needed several cups of coffee to get going.

Chad struggled with this lifestyle for several years. He didn't lose his wife, his kids, or his job, but he gradually lost his self-respect. One day I had lunch with him, and I could tell something had changed. I asked, "What's going on with you?"

He laughed, "Troy, I've made some new decisions. I realized I was poisoning my body with alcohol, caffeine, and sugar . . . and I was slowly poisoning my relationships and my career, too. I used to be happy and confident, but I'd become . . .. I don't know, hard, negative, and moody. A good friend told me I'd better make some changes or I was headed for trouble . . . big trouble. I don't know what you'd call it—turning over a new leaf or something—but it's made a huge difference in my life." Chad paused for second and then a big smile appeared on his face. He told me, "I'm glad you noticed. My wife noticed too. Yesterday she grinned and said, 'It looks like I have my husband back. What took you so long?'"

I had had numerous conversations with Chad over the years, and many times he told me he needed to make major changes—in his consumption of alcohol, his relationships, and how he spent his time—but none of those solemn pronouncements produced lasting change. Like many of us, Chad had to be convinced that his life had run off the rails. Finally, he came to that moment of truth. It was a real turning point.

How wonderful that no one need wait a single moment to improve the world.

—Anne Frank

No more secrets

Kelly and her husband are family friends. Mark is a vice president of an international engineering firm, and he travels more than half of every year. Kelly is a devoted mother to their four children, two in high school and two in junior high. They live in a very nice neighborhood, but Kelly had trouble finding things to fill up her day. To stay busy, she worked for some friends who needed help launching a business, and she volunteered for a number of local charities and agencies. She appeared to be the picture of happiness, but she was often lonely.

When Kelly twisted her back playing tennis, the pain didn't go away with heat, cold, and physical therapy. Her doctor prescribed painkillers, and she discovered they did more than make her back feel better. After a few months her tolerance built up, and she needed a higher dose to dull the pain. More months went by. Kelly wasn't playing tennis, and she didn't feel like volunteering. Her friends were busy and excited about life, but Kelly was spiraling down into depression. After a while, she felt terribly lonely and lost.

When she saw friends who asked how she was doing, she always smiled and insisted, "I'm great! How about you?" But she wasn't doing great, and they knew it. Before long, Kelly was no longer the person everyone wanted to be around; she became someone no one wanted to be around. She desperately tried to hide the secret of her prescription drug addiction, her loneliness, and her growing sense of worthlessness.

Marsha, a friend Kelly hadn't seen in almost a year, called to ask her to go to lunch. After only a few minutes, Marsha realized something was terribly wrong. She began asking questions. When Kelly tried to deflect her probes, Marsha realized her friend was in serious trouble. Her friend's love gave Kelly the security to be honest with someone for the first time in a long time. Gradually, Kelly began to reclaim her life. She found a few others who had struggled, or were struggling, with prescription drugs, and together they found new hope and meaning. Today, Kelly looks like the vibrant, happy person she'd been years before, but now she has far more wisdom and compassion than ever.

Facing facts

Richard is a friend who seemed to have it all. He's smart, handsome, and athletic, with a lovely wife and five kids. I haven't seen his high school yearbook, but I'm sure he was voted "Most Likely to Succeed." He has that air about him. He became an executive in an advertising agency, and he did quite well. He loved to lead meetings of his creative team. He was able to blend enthusiasm, creativity, and brutal honesty about every concept.

Richard often scheduled meetings with his team offsite. To loosen people up and build camaraderie, he brought in beer, Scotch, and the other favorite beverages of his team members. After a while, he added other activities to build team morale, including poker games and regular visits to strip clubs. His company was raking in clients and profits. Richard seemed to be the picture of success.

When Richard got home from conventions or offsite meetings with his team, he lied to his wife to cover up his drinking, gambling, and sexual exploits. He was living a double life. He barely tolerated his dull life at home with his wife and kids, and he longed for the excitement away from home. Gradually, others started to notice the toll his dual lifestyle was taking on him. He gained weight, his language became foul, and some of his best clients began to wonder if Richard was keeping their ad concepts from prying eyes and ears. Before long, no one trusted him.

One Saturday, Richard's best friend asked him to come over to watch a ballgame. When Richard walked into the room, he saw his wife, his siblings, his parents, the president of his company, and a counselor. It was an intervention. Each one told him a version of the same story, "I love you, but I don't know who you are anymore. You need help. If you don't do something, and do it now, your life is going to implode."

Richard was furious and embarrassed, but he realized he was throwing his life away. He checked into a rehab clinic and got the help he needed. The road back included countless apologies and a new set of values to live by. There were a couple of slips along the way, but slowly, Richard rebuilt trust—first with his wife and kids, with the rest of his family, with his boss and the people on his team, and eventually with his clients. He became the likeable, honest, hardworking person he'd been so long before. The prodigal husband, father, son, brother, and coworker had come home.

The future belongs to those who believe in the beauty of their dreams.

—Eleanor Roosevelt

Delayed response

You never know what's going on in people's minds. Years ago I spoke at a major event. In that period of my speaking career, I was very dramatic—and I've always been able to make people laugh. During my talk, the crowd was really into it . . . everyone but one guy sitting on the front row. He just sat and scowled while everyone else howled at my stories and one-liners. I walked over and stood in front of him to see if my next story would get a reaction. When I finished it, everyone around him was laughing, but his face was still made of granite. Not even the faintest smile. Other people were taking notes. He sat with his arms crossed, slouching in his seat with his legs stretched out in front of him. He just sat there. I wondered if we needed to call the coroner.

About ten years later, I was having lunch at an event with a senior executive of one of the biggest and most prestigious companies in the world. A very handsome man walked over to our table, patted the executive on the arm and told him, "Would you mind moving to another table? I'd like to sit next to Troy."

The executive obviously recognized the man. He got up and moved to a nearby table. The man sat next to me, put his arm around my shoulders and said, "You don't remember me, but ten years ago I was in one of your training meetings. Troy, you changed my life."

I immediately realized it was the man who sat so impassively in the front row many years before. He then told me, "The things you said that day have had a massive impact on me and my career. I give you all the credit for helping me grow my business."

I started laughing. I said, "Hey, do you have any idea how hard I was working to connect with you that day? I didn't think I made even a dent!" He smiled, and I then told him, "Do I remember you? Yes, of course. In fact, I'll never forget you as long as I live!"

I still have no idea what was going on in his mind that day years before, but now I don't care. I'm just thrilled that my effort made a difference. Thankfully, this kind of conversation isn't unique. I can't tell you how many times people have told me how my input has had an impact on their careers. I'm always humbled by their stories.

Different lenses

I've heard this story told in different ways by different speakers, but it bears repeating. Two brothers had taken very different paths: one was in prison with a twenty-year sentence and the other was the CEO of a very successful marketing firm. A reporter picked up the story and decided to conduct parallel interviews to see what happened. When he talked to the brother in prison, the reporter asked, "What led to you being here?"

As the man began to speak, bitterness spilled out of every pore. He snarled, "My father beat me, berated me, and he took my dignity and respect from me. Where else would I end up but in prison?"

A few days later in the other brother's corner office, the reporter asked him, "What's the secret of your success?"

The brother took a deep breath and explained, "When I was a boy, my father beat me, berated me, and took my dignity and respect from me. I was determined to make something better of my life. That's how I got here."

Always dream and shoot higher than you know you can do. Do not bother just to be better than your contemporaries or predecessors. Try to be better than yourself.

—**William Faulkner**

A NEW MAP

Let's admit it: we've been afraid to face the hard truths of our heartaches, tension, failure, and stress. It all seems too insurmountable, so we've acted like we're "doing just fine." Sooner or later, all of us hit a wall. I hope you haven't hit one lately, but if you have, you're not alone. The fact is that someone who knows us and loves us is always with us. His constant love gives us the ultimate security so we can be completely honest—with ourselves, with Him, and with at least one other person. Professor and author J.I. Packer assures us:

There is unspeakable comfort . . . in knowing that God is constantly taking knowledge of me in love, and watching over me for my good. There is tremendous relief in knowing that His love to me is utterly realistic, based at every point on prior knowledge of the worst about me, so that no discovery now can disillusion Him about me, in the way that I am so often disillusioned about myself, and quench His determination to bless me.[13]

Some of us have been using the wrong map, after having the right one but losing it. We've been wandering, reacting to every person and each moment, but without any clear plan of where we want our lives to go. Don't wait any longer. Get on a path that promises:

- Your honesty will be rewarded;

- A sense of hope will provide a new direction for your future;

- A clear, workable plan is waiting for you;

- A new sense of confidence will propel you to better things;

- A new security will be a firm foundation for your decisions;

- Challenges will inspire you instead of crushing you;

- Your new hope, confidence, and security will give you peace; and

- You'll live for a purpose far bigger than yourself.

Be ruthlessly objective about the patterns of behavior in your life, and make changes before you dig a deep hole of dumb decisions and passive responses. But even if you've dug a deep hole and your list of bad choices looks like a New York City phone book, you can still have a bright future.

No matter how far you've fallen, no matter how blind you've been, no matter how many lives you've messed up or how much trouble you're in, it's never too late to change directions, to find hope, and to get on a path toward peace and purpose.

If the people in these stories can do it, you can do it. If I can do it, you can do it.

-------------------- ❖ --------------------

Who is the happier man, he who has braved the storm of life and lived or he who has stayed securely on shore and merely existed?

—Hunter S. Thompson

THINK ABOUT IT . . .

1. What are some reasons that being honest about our stresses and failures is so hard? Why is it essential?

2. What happens when we have insight but we fail to take action?

3. Which of the stories about second chances resonates with you? Explain your answer.

4. In what way is prolonged helplessness the ultimate escape and an excuse for not taking courageous steps toward peace and purpose?

5. So, is change a pipedream for you? Why or why not?

CHAPTER 4 | MIND GAMES

If you have a purpose in which you can believe, there's no end to the amount of things you can accomplish.

—Marian Anderson

For the first twenty to twenty-five years of my career, I was the master of positive self-talk. I read affirming, visionary authors, and I grabbed inspiring quotes to energize me through each day. I constantly listened to motivational messages, first on cassette tapes, then on CDs, and most recently on podcast. Waking or sleeping, I was always reading or listening to positive messages. In this process, I became astute at recognizing negative messages that swirled in my head, such as "I'm a loser," "This can't work," "I'm going to fail . . . again," and "What if people really knew me?" I grabbed those thoughts, wrestled them out of my brain, and threw them in the garbage heap of mental trash. Then I replaced them with the positive messages I'd read that day or remembered from past reading.

For me (and I suspect, for every other person on the planet), replacing negative messages with positive ones is a moment-by-moment struggle, a constant fight. I slipped dozens of times a day and let the poisonous thoughts grab me for a minute (or maybe an hour), but I developed enough mental strength to wage a fairly consistent fight.

During those years, I also became a student of the messages coming out of other people's mouths. I noticed that many people, from top executives to those with the most menial jobs, were what I called "positive-negative" people. When I first met someone, or during the first few minutes of a conversation with old acquaintances, they smiled and acted like they were on top of the world. They tried to project a positive, can-do image. Before long, however, their pent-up doubts, criticisms, blame, and fear began to leak out—and if I listened long enough, the drips sometimes became a torrent!

My observations of others caused me to continually evaluate the messages projected from my facial expressions, my tone of voice, and the words I articulated. I didn't want to be a positive-negative person. I wanted to be someone who was very realistic about problems, but just as tenaciously hopeful in pursuing solutions. That's a person who is secure and confident. That's a person who isn't sour and doesn't panic. That's a person who brings light and life to every encounter.

No matter how noble our intentions may be, it only takes one discouraging area of life to cloud a person's thinking and turn an upbeat, optimistic person into a complaining, blaming, gloomy pessimist. For instance, a top athlete, maybe someone who competes in the decathlon in the Olympics, smashes his thumb with a hammer. He's still incredibly fit, with all the potential in the world to do amazing things in track and field, but his entire attention is suddenly riveted on his throbbing thumb. Nothing else in the world matters, and for him, nothing else in the world exists!

Hope begins in the dark, the stubborn hope that if you just show up and try to do the right thing, the dawn will come.

—Anne Lamott

A few years ago, I was like that Olympic athlete—not in athletic prowess, but in letting one small area of life consume and cloud my entire perspective. My insurance business was growing and expanding, my speaking schedule was as full as I wanted it to be, and my consulting work was enjoyable, stimulating, and lucrative. But a few stupid financial decisions became almost the only thing I thought about. I blamed myself for being so stupid, and I blamed any partners in those deals for not foreseeing the problems. I worried about the mounting debts in those ancillary business ventures, and I let all those fears and doubts dominate my thoughts.

I suspect each of us has a tender spot, an aspect of our lives that is particularly vulnerable. Even if everything else in our lives is going exceptionally well, failure in this area—or even the threat of failure—turns our minds into toxic waste dumps. For many of us, the tender spot is our family relationships. No matter how successful we are in business, unresolved conflict at home crushes our spirits. We either get no pleasure out of our business performance, or we escape into our work and try to ignore the problems at home. Either way leads to more heartache.

When failure or loss in our most vulnerable area threatens to turn us into perpetual pessimists, we need to do something about it. The remedy varies depending on the situation. Relational strains need to be exposed, addressed, and healed through forgiveness given and forgiveness received. Then, and only then, can trust be rebuilt—and trust is the essential glue in any meaningful relationship.

In addition, other mental toxins may result from problems with health issues, finances, kids, in-laws, sex, or a dozen other major categories. All of them had specific causes, so all of them have specific solutions—not easy solutions, but processes that promise the restoration of peace and purpose.

In my case, the solution was to eliminate my investments in bad business deals and stop getting into new ones. I sold my interest in virtually every venture that isn't in the sweet spot of my business career. In some cases, I had to take a significant loss to get out, but it was worth it. Peace of mind is far more valuable than some vain hope that a bad investment will magically turn around and make a profit. The one exception I made was for my restaurant, but I found a supremely competent person, my brother Keith, to be my partner. It has proven to be the right solution in that particular case. I'm no longer emotionally distraught or tied to the ups and downs of that enterprise. I've found a trustworthy person to take care of all the details, which has let me step away and regain my sanity.

Before we reallocate our finances, make major business decisions, or try to rectify a difficult relationship, we need to acknowledge the games we're playing in our minds. If we don't learn to fill our minds with positive, helpful, hope-filled thoughts, we'll almost certainly go off track—or never get on track to begin with. As always, change begins with an accurate analysis.

The realist sees reality as concrete. The optimist sees reality as clay.

—Robert Brault

THE PLAGUE

Most of the people who have met me during my career would never guess that much of my success has been driven by self-doubt. I was so committed to be successful because I was terrified of failing. From the day the company took away my subsidy program and my safety net, I lived under a cloud. The circumstances may be far different from one person to another, but I believe all of us wrestle with a normal, pervasive human condition: the plague of radical insecurity. Some are pretty good at hiding it under a veneer of good looks, titles, awards, verbal acuity, and the flash of owning nice things, and virtually all of us try to hide it in one way or another. But if we remove our masks of social niceties and are brutally honest, we'll admit much of what we do is driven by our desperate desire to cover up our flaws and present ourselves as valuable. In essence, we're marketing ourselves to each other. (Of course, sociopaths and narcissists don't struggle with an innate sense of insecurity, but they create far bigger problems—mostly in the lives of those who try to relate to them.)

As much as we try to mask insecurity, it comes out in our thinking, and then, often barely filtered, in our words, gestures, and actions. Let me describe some of the toxic messages that often lurk in our minds.

"I should have . . ."

These are often the opening words of statements of regret. When we say, "I should have," we lament that we're too late to make a difference. We've let an opportunity pass us by, or we let down someone we love.

"I ought to . . ."

This sentiment isn't about regretting the past; it's a fear of the future. Sometimes, it's a declaration of intent to reach a goal, which is perfectly good and right. But often, these words are tinged with self-doubt, the dread that we won't measure up to the challenge.

Twenty years from now you will be more disappointed by the things you didn't do than by the ones you did do. So throw off the bowlines. Sail away from the safe harbor. Catch the trade winds in your sail. Explore. Dream. Discover.

—Mark Twain

"I'm not as good as . . ."

We often think comparison is simply a part of normal, healthy life, but it can be insidious and dangerous. When we compare ourselves unfavorably—"I'm not as smart as, as competent as, as pretty as, as gifted as, etc.,"—we see clearly that it produces a negative evaluation that may, in fact, be accurate. However, these conclusions are often stated (and thought) without context. It would be much healthier to think, "I'm not as smart as Jim, but I work hard, and I have a bright future in the company."

Even positive comparison can have a negative edge. If a parent says, "You're a better athlete (or student or dancer or whatever) than your brother," the not-so-subtle message is, "You'd better perform, or I'll be criticizing you in front of others!" Parents, leaders, and managers may think they're pumping people up by favorable comparison, but they're actually reinforcing the perception that failure will have tragic results. Positive comparison produces pride at first, but it soon instills fear. It's far better to compare a person's performance with his or her own past performance: "You're doing so much better than you did last month. Way to go!"

"I'm a victim."

In every culture and in every age, injustice is a reality. Ours is no different. Many people are, in fact, victims of abuse, abandonment, manipulation, and all kinds of other hurts. They were victimized, but they don't have to assume the permanent identity of a victim. People who see themselves as perpetually helpless victims are demanding. They insist that others pay for offenses—they want revenge! They insist on compensation for the losses they have been dealt, and they want guarantees that it will never happen again. Their demands simply are unrealistic, making them vulnerable to being let down by those who don't give them everything they want—which includes the entire population of the planet.

People who see themselves as victims don't grieve their wounds, forgive, and move on with life. Instead, they hold grudges. They get their sense of identity from being "the one who was wronged," and they feel a surge of energy every day from their adrenaline-fueled resentment.

"This is the worst!"

A form of very destructive self-talk occurs when a person assumes any and every problem is the ultimate apocalypse. Psychologists call this "catastrophizing" or "awfulizing." You probably know people who do this. Something difficult happens at home or at work, and the person's negative assessment jumps from 0 to 10 in a heartbeat. Instead of "This isn't good, but we'll find a way through it," the person explodes, "This is a calamity! My world will never be the same!" The person may also project the results of Armageddon onto a person who made a bad decision. If a daughter is seen hanging out with a boy with a bad reputation, the parent may erupt, "Just think of what your life will become. Other people will think you're worthless, and your life will be ruined!"

This kind of thinking is unrestrained fear on steroids! The rest of us may shake our heads and wonder how the person could draw such drastic conclusions, but to the deeply distressed person, the calamitous assumptions make perfect sense.

"You always . . ." or "You never . . ."

One way to avoid hard decisions is to make them easier by painting them as black and white—situations are "all good" or "all bad," and people are "always" trustworthy or "never" come through when we need them. Extreme, all-encompassing statements are rarely factual. Sure, a situation may be difficult, but courage and hope can usually enable us to find nuggets of gold in the dirt of life. And a person may lie, but that doesn't mean everything he says is a lie. When we make people into two-dimensional, cartoon characters—"He's a liar!"—we may feel better for the moment, but we've effectively blocked any chance of communication and ruined the opportunity to find common ground.

"I can top that."

Early in my career, when people asked me how I was doing, I always gave the same response: "Awesome!" Everything, every time, everywhere was always "awesome!" In fact, people started calling me "Mr. Awesome." I wanted to be positive, but to keep up my persona, I couldn't admit anything was less than fabulous . . . so I stretched the truth. If something was good, I made it a little bit better. If I told a good story about a failure, I made it a little worse than it was. I was a master at the fine art of exaggeration. If anyone called me out on something I said, I could backpedal or obfuscate with the best of them. None of my statements were horrendous, bald-faced lies, but they were exaggerations. And exaggerations are a form of lying.

Why do we exaggerate? It's simple: to make ourselves look a little bit better, and to make others look a little worse. It's fear-driven jockeying for position.

Whatever is at the center of our life will be the source of our security, guidance, wisdom, and power.

—Stephen Covey

The problem with all of these toxic messages is that everyone's pattern of thinking—even the most self-destructive and vision-killing thinking—seems absolutely, completely, perfectly normal. It's the way we've thought for years, and until we step back and take a long, hard look at the messages in our minds each day, we'll just let them keep running loose and doing their damage.

If we can step out of our heads from time to time and hold our thoughts in our hands, so to speak, we can then choose to keep the good ones and throw the rest away. We don't have to let negative thoughts continue to plague our lives. We can choose a more positive mindset.

Seth Godin is an author, speaker, and entrepreneur. He observed, "Optimism is the most important human trait, because it allows us to evolve our ideas, to improve our situation, and to hope for a better tomorrow."[14]

We also need to remember that when dealing with others, our language and tone of voice can make a big difference. When I'm upset, my words can have an edge—and sometimes their impact can bludgeon people. When I'm discouraged or worried or angry, I can say the right things, but my tone of voice and facial expressions scream something much different. It's not enough for me to be civil; I need to be both truthful and kind at the same time. And I need to let my face know what my heart wants to communicate.

THE ART OF FILTERING

In my life and in this book, I'm striving to be a more genuine, honest person. Part of this commitment means that I try to notice when I'm marketing myself, exaggerating to impress people, blaming people for my mistakes, or playing any of the other mind games I've just described. I'm not claiming to have arrived, but I'm committed to changing the game. My internal filter used to be geared to present myself in the most favorable light. My new filter is based on a greater sense of security, peace, and purpose, so I can afford to just be Troy . . . warts and all, without pretense and without shame.

Let me offer some suggestions as you analyze, select, filter, and replace the thoughts in your mind each day.

Look at your source of security.

If your identity is based on your performance, your appearance, your intellect, or anything that can be challenged or taken away, you'll always ride the roller coaster of pride when you're doing well and shame when you're not. In the first chapter, I explained that I've found a source outside myself: the love, forgiveness, and acceptance of God by the grace poured out on me in Jesus Christ. You may find the same source, or you may find a very different one, but find one that captures your heart, one that amazes you, and one that becomes an immovable rock where you can stand when the floods of life rage.

Find the courage to be vulnerable.

Without security, we're either fiercely guarded because we don't trust people with the secrets of our hearts, or we may foolishly trust the wrong people, get hurt again, and then withdraw into a shell of hurt and fear. As we grow in our security, however, we need to find at least one person, maybe two or three, who are safe, wise, and strong. With them, we can share our deepest longing, our highest hopes, and our secret fears. It's amazing what happens when we find someone like this. We can relax, we realize we don't have to hide, and we don't have to compulsively tell strangers how we feel about life. In this relationship, we'll gain a wealth of insight and strength.

Analyze patterns and specifics of thoughts.

In some ways, this is the easiest thing in the world to do. As you read the descriptions of the mind games in this chapter, which ones hit you like a truck? Those are probably ingrained thought patterns you've used for decades. Change is a process.

Let me illustrate how it works: I've said that exaggerating the truth was a subconscious pattern in my life. After I became aware of this habit, I began to notice my expansion of the truth as the words came out of my mouth. I thought, *Oh, I did it again!* Yet recognition *after the fact* was the first step of progress. Then I tried to detect the thoughts earlier, when they were in my mind *before* I said the words. Sometimes I succeeded and changed my statement before I spoke, but sometimes I still said the words and caught myself later. That's okay; that's progress, too. Over time, I've learned to *anticipate the tendency* and choose the rock-hard truth before I enter a conversation. To be honest, I still fight the urge to exaggerate, but at least I no longer glory in it! That's what analysis and change looks like for me.

Get plenty of the right fuel.

As my source of security has changed, I've realized I need a lot more input to reinforce my new views about life. I'd read hundreds, maybe thousands of books about business success, but I began reading much more about finding my security in God's grace. My mother gave me a daily devotional called *Jesus Calling*,[15] a book that injects this truth into my mind and heart every day. I also read books by insightful, inspiring leaders who point me to the blessings we've received from God. The more I read, the hungrier I've become to know more, learn more, and love more.

Of course, modern technology provides many more options to expose us to encouraging, challenging, and inspiring messages. Today, you can download books on your iPad and iPhone, and Google offers a variety of ways to access books, music, and mp3 files of your favorite speakers.

Now when I read books or listen to talks about business strategies, I have different presuppositions. Instead of implementing the strategies in an attempt to become more valuable and secure, I can implement them from a foundation of security. Then, success is a joy, not a way to show I'm better than others. And failure is just a momentary setback, not a threat to my identity.

As a side benefit of reading inspirational books, I've memorized statements and Bible verses, often without even trying. They've meant so much to me that I simply can't stop thinking about them. All of us need a lot of inspiring, positive raw material to regularly inject into our minds.

You're a leader. It's your job to keep your passion hot. Do whatever you have to do, read whatever you have to read, go wherever you have to go to stay fired up. And don't apologize to anybody.

—Bill Hybels

Use every moment.

Modern technology makes it possible to listen to the greatest teachers and inspirational leaders in the world—at any time of the day or night. I used to worry about all kinds of things as I rode in my car or sat at the airport, but I now plug in my mp3 player and listen to fantastic speakers from all over the country. I still spend plenty of time planning for my business and my personal life, but I desperately need the motivational shot in the arm these leaders give me during my down time each day.

Be patient and persistent.

Training a dog requires time, energy, and patience. Retraining a mind takes even more of these qualities! It's easy to get discouraged when our thoughts don't change as quickly as we hoped, but we need to realize that we're doing the hard work of reframing years, perhaps decades, of ingrained patterns of thinking. Keep feeding your mind with uplifting, hope-drenched thoughts, find a person or two to join you on the journey, and look for the positives in your relationships, your career, and all of your life.

When I approached the pits of despair a few years ago, I thought I was going insane. At times a line from a Bob Dylan song would get stuck in my mind. All I could think about was, "You don't need a weatherman to know which way the wind blows."[16] The words made me feel stupid, self-absorbed, and ashamed. Why hadn't I seen what was coming? Why had I been so blind? I became so obsessed with this lyric that I couldn't think about anything else, and I couldn't go to sleep. I also had flashbacks of the movie, *A Beautiful Mind*, and I thought, *That's me! I'm just as crazy as John Nash!*

I had to force myself to fill my mind with something besides self-blame and worry, so I picked up books to read. I especially benefited from reading biographies about Walt Disney and Richard Nixon, two men who were haunted by self-doubt and driven to do something great. They were flawed but brilliant, and somehow, their examples gave me hope.

TAKE ACTION

A few years ago, I attended a remarkable event. Anthony Galie is a psychotherapist, author, and speaker, but on this night I saw another amazing talent: he's a hypnotist with extraordinary talents. As part of his show, he asked the audience to complete some statements. He casually stated, "Winston tastes good . . ." and the crowd roared, "Like a cigarette should!" Then he said, "Don't squeeze . . ." and the audience shouted, "The Charmin!"

He explained that the mind is an incredibly powerful computer. Neither of those (or the other ads he related to audience members that night) had been used in the media for decades,[17] but they were still deeply embedded in our minds.[18]

Other messages from our pasts are also deeply embedded in our subconscious minds, with far more significance than cigarettes, toilet paper, cars, or soda. They speak to the core of our identity, our worth as human beings, and our value to others. The thoughts rambling through our minds each day have been put there by the people we love and the people who have hurt us—our best experiences and our worst pains. Some of them thrill us, but many haunt us. The point is that we don't have to let them control us any longer. We've seen that change requires more than good intentions; it demands action.

Change is hard because people overestimate the value of what they have—and underestimate the value of what they may gain by giving that up.

—James Belasco and Ralph Stayer

Put some (or all) of these suggestions into action:

- Find a teacher or speaker who inspires you, and download talks.

- Set up your phone or mp3 player in your car so you can listen to the messages as you drive to and from work, or listen to them as you exercise.

- Find a devotional and other inspiring books to read. You can ask people to give them to you for Christmas or your birthday, but don't wait: get the first one immediately, and start reading.

- Write positive statements on cards and put them on your mirror, in your wallet or purse, or next to your computer.

- For a week, set your watch or phone timer to go off at least three times a day. Each time it does, analyze your thoughts. What are you thinking about? If you're having negative, self-defeating thoughts, don't beat yourself up for. Acknowledge each one, and look for patterns. My guess is that the same ones recur over and over again.

- Watch the words that come out of your mouth. Try to catch critical statements, lies, cursing, and exaggerations before you say them.

- Whenever you have a negative thought or word, immediately replace it with a truth you've learned from a book, a devotional, or a message.

- If you struggle to make progress, don't quit. You're trying to overcome many years of entrenched patterns of thought.

- Find a friend who's on the same journey of replacing toxic thoughts with uplifting ones, and regularly encourage each other.

As I've tried to make these changes, I've realized that my harsh, negative language hurt other people because they had to hear it, but it also had a destructive impact on me because it reinforced my critical perspective. Change requires hard work, but it's possible . . . and changing the messages in our minds and mouths pays great dividends in every part of our lives.

CLOSE THE LOOP

One of the most powerful ways to change the negativity in our minds is to speak positive messages to the people around us. If noticing the positive traits of others doesn't come naturally (that is, if you're a grouch!), you'll need to do some hard work. Most of us, though, just need to open our eyes to notice and then open our mouths to say, "Way to go!" "That's a great insight!" or "Thank you so much!" Some of us have used words to control others for a long, long time; changing our messages will work wonders in our relationships.

We simply can't find peace of mind and live for a transcendent purpose if we keep thinking the same destructive thoughts. The battle for the future is between your ears. Fight hard, and don't give up.

Laugh at yourself, but don't ever aim your doubt at yourself. Be bold. When you embark for strange places, don't leave any of yourself safely on shore. Have the nerve to go into unexplored territory.

—Alan Alda

THINK ABOUT IT . . .

1. How would you describe the attitude, perceptions, and communication of a "positive-negative person"?

2. Which kind of "toxic messages" resonated with you? How do they affect your self-concept, your relationships, and your goals?

3. Why is the source of our security so important in shaping the thoughts in our minds?

4. How would you describe the process of developing a new habit of thinking and speaking positive messages?

5. Write a plan to take at least three action steps to change your thought patterns, and thereby change your life.

CHAPTER 5 | VITAL CONNECTIONS

The greatest sweetener of human life is friendship. To raise this to the highest pitch of enjoyment is a secret which but few discover.

—Joseph Addison

When unrelieved stress has eroded our peace and purpose, we can often point to bad decisions we've made in our relationships. The restoration of a clear and peaceful mind and a compelling sense that our lives matter doesn't happen in isolation. We need a few wise, strong people who have walked the path we need to walk. If we look back on our lives, we'll see givers and takers. I've had my share.

GIVERS

My mother, Iva Korsgaden, is the quintessential example of a giver. I don't know where I'd be today without her love, strength, support, and encouragement. My father died tragically in a car accident when I was five years old. My mother came home from the funeral and saw five children she needed to raise on her own. I'm the middle of the pack. I have two older brothers and two younger sisters. That day she decided to devote the rest of her life to the five of us, to pour as much love, wisdom, and hope into us as she could find within her—and it turned out that she had a wealth of those wonderful qualities!

One of the things I admire about my mother is that she has a very strong faith in God, and she's not judgmental toward others in the least. When I was growing up, I didn't understand how rare it is for someone to be convinced he's right without condemning others for being wrong. She beautifully blends confidence and compassion.

My mom could easily have been overwhelmed by the lonely responsibility of raising her five kids, but she was amazingly cheerful. We had a schedule that provided stability in the home. She cooked breakfast every morning and made sack lunches for us, and she was at the door when we came home from school every afternoon. She encouraged us to play any sport we enjoyed, and she was our biggest cheerleader. My siblings were gifted athletes, but I wasn't. Still, my mother encouraged me to get involved in something meaningful after school.

Every night at the dinner table we had spirited discussions about any and every topic. Nothing, it seems, was off limits. The debates were often quite heated, and no one held back. Everyone had a point, and all of us were determined to be heard in every discussion. Visitors probably felt a little uncomfortable because most families aren't as open and honest, but we loved it. We could disagree with each other without a hint of condemnation. We had a blast. On Sunday nights the six of us gathered in the living room and turned on the black-and-white television to watch "The Wonderful World of Disney." We were very close, and we still are.

Amazingly, my mother made a point of spending time with each of us individually. When I was just a little boy, she took me to McDonald's to give me focused attention. It was a big deal because we didn't have much money to spare, but she wanted to do things with and for each of us to communicate that we were special. The hamburgers were fifteen cents. My mother took great delight in treating me. We never had to wonder about the depth, tenderness, or tenacity of our mother's love for us.

My mom is a remarkable person. She was a single mother who devoted her life to her children and was thoroughly involved in our lives without a shred of self-pity. I never heard her complain about the hand life had dealt her. To compensate for the deficit of being fatherless, she made sure all her children were involved in activities led by good men. Because of her influence, I never had any sense that my life was lacking anything, even though my father died when I was so young.

People in the community have seen the way my mother treated her kids, and they admire her. They see that she's a very special person. She gave me a firm foundation. Every day, in all the highs and lows of life, I look back and appreciate my mother's example, her love and laughter, and the wisdom she imparted to us. Even today, she still speaks words of hope and vision into my life. If she weren't my mother, I'd still recommend her for "World's Greatest Mom."

Intimate attachments to other human beings are the hub around which a person's life revolves.

—John Bowlby

When I was in middle school, one of my music teachers was Joe Hannah, who would become one of the singers in a group called Sons of the San Joaquin, which specialized in western music. At the time he was the leader of the men's chorus at the school as well as a coach for the football and baseball teams. I played on one of Mr. Hannah's teams at the school, but I wasn't a stellar athlete. It was clear I didn't have a future in Major League Baseball or the NFL. With his encouragement, I joined the choir at school. As you might imagine, there weren't many young men in the school choir, but I soon began to experience the positive impact of a very different set of Mr. Hannah's talents.

Joe was a man's man. He had been an all-star baseball player; he was handsome. One day after practice he pulled me aside and said, "Troy, I know your mom and your older brothers. I believe you can play a big role in convincing other boys to join the choir. I know it's not seen as the cool thing to do, but if *you're* involved, people will take notice. You know a lot of the athletes at the school. If you invite them to join the choir, they might come. Will you help me?"

I was glad to help. I invited several friends from various sports teams to come, and a few of them joined the choir. Joe made it so much fun. We sang a lot of popular and western songs, and we loved it. Joe's demeanor was very positive. He won everyone's admiration and respect, but he was no pushover. He even had a positive impact on a number of the troubled kids who drove the other teachers crazy.

Joe Hannah showed me that real men don't have to follow a narrowly prescribed path to success. And real men genuinely care about others. When I spent time with him, I thought, *Wow, I want to be like this guy!* I still think of him often.

After I graduated from high school, I thought I was a gifted musician and singer. I planned to make a career in the music business, so I moved to the Los Angeles area to begin making a splash. When I got there and began to audition, I realized I had a lot of competition because many of the most gifted artists in the country come to Los Angeles. Actually, I soon discovered there wasn't as much competition as I first thought. Almost every other singer and musician—I played piano and guitar—was far better than me! It was obvious that my future in music had hit a quick dead end.

I tried a couple of jobs in Los Angeles, but they didn't seem very promising so I decided to move back to my hometown of Visalia, California, to see if I could find something better. I knew some people in the insurance business. I called the district manager for Farmers Insurance, Jay Green, and asked to meet with him. He told me about the company and showed me a video about selling insurance. When he finished, I told him, "Sir, if you hire me, I'll make you rich." He didn't laugh, and he didn't even smile. He hired me on the spot.

Years later, Jay told me the company rated new hires either A, B, C, or D. After the interview, he had rated me a D, the lowest level of qualifications for an agent. He also said that he hired me only because he felt pressure to meet a company quota. If he hadn't hired me, he was going to be in big trouble. It wasn't an auspicious beginning.

I worked in Jay's office for nine years. I saw him in the best times and the worst times. Jay was a wonderful man and a terrific boss. He adored his wife and loved his kids. His authentic, positive personality was magnetic, and he lived the principles and priorities I'm describing in this book. He modeled a joy-filled, love-filled life of meaning and purpose. He was also very inquisitive. When new ideas came through the company pipeline, he didn't immediately reject them simply because they were new. He studied them and tried to figure out how his customers could benefit.

When the computer revolution was in its infancy, Jay was on the forefront of the wave. He was excited about the possibilities of using a computer to provide better service and keep up with the mass of data that flows into and out of agency offices. By then, he was getting older and nearing retirement, but he had the enthusiasm and openness of a twenty year old. Jay also had a great sense of humor. He sometimes wore overalls with a sport coat when he went to the corporate office. The people who didn't know him stared and wondered who in the world this hayseed could be. His friends just laughed and shook their heads. Somehow, Jay combined professionalism with humor.

As my business grew, I still had my office with Jay. In fact, I crammed nine people into three cramped little rooms in his office. The agency was managing thousands of policies and growing like crazy. Other mentors might have been threatened by the success of their protégé, but Jay reveled in my success. He was as thrilled as I was. He often patted me on the back and grinned, "Troy, I'm so proud of you!"

Later, when companies began asking me to speak at their events, I often invited Jay to come with me. He sat in the audience and beamed as I spoke. I can't tell you how much his love and support has meant to me. When I think back on those first nine years, I realize I wasn't the easiest guy in the world to lead. I made plenty of mistakes. When I lost my subsidy program, I thought my career had washed out, but Jay gave me another chance. In fact, he gave me more than a chance; he gave me confidence that I could make it.

People with deep and lasting friendships may be introverts, extroverts, young, old, dull, intelligent, homely, good-looking; but the one characteristic they always have in common is openness.

—Alan Loy McGinnis

I had the good fortune of meeting two legends in the insurance industry. Jack and Garry Kinder, better known as "The Kinder Brothers," were experts on life insurance and financial services. Early in my career as I started to achieve success, they were gracious enough to spend time with me. They invited me to meet with them in their offices in Dallas—no charge, just freely giving their time to help me. Jack and Garry didn't focus our conversations only on insurance; they coached me to be a well-rounded person.

Jack and Garry played ball when they were young. They were great coaches, and like Joe Hannah, they had the ability to help people see a bigger picture. A number of other people gave generously of their time and expertise, and I'll always be grateful for all of them. However, Jack and Garry Kinder poured into my life from the beginning, and they didn't ask for a thing. They just gave, invested, and cared. They are two of the finest people I've ever known. Garry is still living, and I consider him my mentor and a close friend to our family and me.

A number of other people have been treasured gifts to me. My brothers and sisters have always been incredibly supportive. My wife and children have loved me in the good times and during my struggles. Mike Robertson (my pastor), Sam Chand, and many others have been close friends and valued mentors for me. I know I can call any of these people at any time for any reason, and they'll be there for me. They're givers. I'm blessed and overflowing because of these people, and I could mention many more.

You don't need a hundred givers in your life, but you desperately need a few. They're worth more than gold.

We need camaraderie, affection, love. These are not options in life, or sentimental trimmings; they are part of our species' survival kit. We need to belong.

—Les and Leslie Parrott

TAKERS

Many people had a very different childhood from mine. All of us have heard horror stories of abuse and abandonment, of addictions and the impact of divorce on children, of death and sickness. Some of those deep wounds are unavoidable: tragic accidents, acts of nature, contagious diseases. But other hurts are caused by deliberate acts of selfishness. The people who hurt us can be called many things. I'm calling them "takers" because they've taken something valuable from us: innocence, safety, love, security, happiness, or something else that can't be replaced.

Thankfully, the takers in my life aren't from my family, although I've had plenty from other sources. In many cases, people see my success and try to use me as a stepstool to reach higher in their lives and careers. Regularly, people call me and "volunteer" to speak at events where I'm speaking, or they ask me to make some calls to set up speaking engagements at major companies for them. Some of them expect to be paid what I'm paid, but they haven't put in the years of work to earn credibility.

Don't get me wrong. I want to be like Jay Green and be thrilled with the success of others, but it doesn't do them any good to make their way too easy. Jay was proud of me because I worked hard and slowly built my business and my credibility. I expect the same from others.

I've also had business partners outside the insurance industry who have taken advantage of me. I've lost a world of money because I trusted the wrong people. Maybe I should have noticed the clues earlier, or maybe the pressures and temptations that surfaced as the deals developed turned honorable people into unscrupulous ones. I don't know, but in my relationships with these people, their taking has included a lot of dollars, and in many cases, I've also suffered blows to my reputation.

Actually, I've met very few people who meant to hurt me. Psychologists estimate that two to three percent of men and less than one percent of women are sociopaths, so fewer than one out of fifty people we meet has "arrested moral development."[19] The rest are just a little bit selfish, a little bit foolish, and a little bit scared. That's why most people do dumb things that hurt others.

Secure, mature, healthy people don't make too many assumptions when I meet with them. They have reasonable requests, they ask very good questions, and they listen to my answers. But difficult people, the takers, ask for the moon, make demands, and ask only when I'm going to come through for them. They aren't good listeners because they don't want to hear any of my reservations.

Takers come in many forms and levels of intensity. Some just annoy us, but others devastate us. To some degree, they all erode our peace of mind because they inject uncertainty, worry, and fear into our thoughts.

As I mentioned, some of the pain we experience is beyond our ability to protect ourselves from it, but other wounds occur because we've been naïve or foolish. The person did and said things that hurt us because we put ourselves in a position to be hurt. We may have trusted someone who is known for dishonesty. That's on us.

God gives us our relatives—thank God we can choose our friends.

—Ethel Watts Mumford

Why do we do such things? Why don't we see trouble coming and prevent the trauma? Let me offer a few possible answers to these perplexing questions.

First, many of us have a natural, human, compassionate desire to help others. We see someone in need, and we dive in to meet the need. In our instinct to help, however, we overlook warning signs. We take responsibility for things the other person should be responsible for, and we get too much of a thrill out of being a hero.

Second, we may be too easily persuaded. I've talked to plenty of great salesmen, but I still sometimes fall for a slick presentation. We don't just want things to work out well; we want things to work out *incredibly* well! So we lower our guard and believe the unbelievable. From the right salesman at the right time, over-promising sounds completely convincing.

The third reason is closely related to the second: we want the easy money. We hear stories about someone investing a few dollars in an invention and making millions, investing a few years in a company and building it into a conglomerate, or winning the lottery. We think, *Why not me?* Greed blinds us. Oh, we don't want to call it greed, but that's what it is. The thirst for the quick hit, the easy money, the big deal makes us vulnerable to deception and subsequently, huge financial losses. The most fundamental dictum in investing is, "If it looks too good to be true . . ."

Finally, some of us have a simple, open, generous personality. Such people make wonderful friends, but they are vulnerable to being taken by an unscrupulous person in business. Generosity is a wonderful trait, but it needs to be combined with shrewdness. Jesus told His followers, "Be as shrewd as snakes and harmless as doves" (Matt. 10:16). That's an essential combination.

We can't stop all hurts and disappointments from coming into our lives, but we can stop being as foolish, as arrogant, as greedy, and as naïve as we've been before. I have to take deep, long looks into the patterns of my life to see these various ways I let people hurt me. Then, and only then, can I do something about them.

Often we have no time for our friends but all the time in the world for our enemies.

—Leon Uris

THE RIGHT KIND OF TRUST

Trust is the glue of relationships. When it's present and strong, our relationships can withstand the storms of life. When it's shaky, even the smallest problems look like Mt. Everest. We can make a number of mistakes in our trust of others. Some of us trust blindly; we trust even untrustworthy people. At a subconscious level, we've calculated that confronting the person will be too threatening, too awkward, too isolating for us to bear, so we put our heads in the sand and act like everything's okay.

Others are on the other end of the spectrum. They've been hurt so badly or so often in the past that they hide behind impenetrable steel walls in their hearts. They're unwilling to take the risk to trust anybody any time, even those who are imminently trustworthy. Their relationships are superficial, and they run from even the slightest risk of exposure because any exposure might bring another devastating hurt.

Still others don't trust anyone, but their fear response is different from those who hide. These people, too, have been wounded in the past, and they're determined not to let anyone hurt them ever again. They're compelled to always be one-up, dominant, in control, and fiercely independent. Instead of being passive and withdrawn, they're aggressive. Quite often, these people are charming much of the time . . . until they feel threatened. Then they pull out the verbal knives and cut people to shreds! They're not going to lose!

Genuine trust is always earned and is based on a long history of proven integrity. It's a beautiful thing. Wise and strong people are able to ask hard questions, listen intently, be appropriately vulnerable, and move forward with their eyes wide open. Sometimes they realize the person they've trusted isn't as honorable or as thorough as they had assumed. They don't react by hiding, making foolish assumptions, or attacking. Instead, they engage in honest, respectful, solution-focused conversation to work through the problem. If they resolve the difficulty together, another brick is cemented to the foundation of a good relationship based on honesty and trust.

In a few relationships in my life, the people I trust and who trust me don't have to give any reasons, excuses, or answers. If we want to explain what we've done and why we've done it, that's fine, but our trust is so deep and strong that no words are necessary.

In business, families, friendships, and other meaningful human interaction, we usually come to one another with our own assumptions about people in general, and perhaps, about the other person in particular. If we tend to trust too much, we need to ask harder questions and only believe people when their actions match their verbal commitments. If we've hidden in fear, we need to find at least one safe person and take a step at a time to become more open. If we've intimidated people to control them and used charm to disarm them, we need to find a new source of security so we can truly care about people instead of manipulating them for our gain.

We all make mistakes in relationships, but I've made far too many. In some cases, the red lights were flashing on the crossing gate, but I was asleep at the wheel. I barreled on into a deal or a hire without ever noticing the plain warning signs. But difficulties in relationships haven't always been due to my lack of diligence. Some people have been very good at deceiving others, including me, and in some cases, they just dropped the ball without any hint of evil intent.

In my book *Power Position Your Agency*, I suggested taking kids to work and making family members an integral part of your business. This strategy certainly worked for me, but I've also heard horror stories from leaders who hired family members who proved to be incompetent or disruptive . . . or both. Whether or not our staff members are relatives, finding and keeping the right people are imperative.

In *Good to Great,* Jim Collins' research of the leaders of the very best companies showed that hiring the right people is imperative to our success *and* our sanity. He summarized his extended interviews with presidents and CEOs by using the metaphor of a bus: The goal of leaders, he explains, is to get the wrong people off the bus, the right people on, and put them in the right seats. Only then, he asserts, can the company (or division or department or team) accomplish great things.[20]

We might paraphrase Collins's observation: Hire for character, and train for competence. I completely agree with this concept, but with a few exceptions. If you're hiring someone to run a nuclear power plant or to be the CFO of your company, you'll need to value competence and experience very highly, without ever taking character for granted. (Actually, competence without character is very dangerous. A skilled but unscrupulous person can ruin a company or blow up a nuclear power plant!) Trust is always earned. Character is paramount, but our employees continue to build their "trust accounts" with us as they display a blend of integrity and expertise.

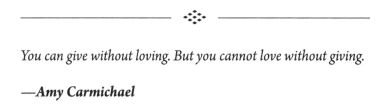

You can give without loving. But you cannot love without giving.

—*Amy Carmichael*

SURROUND YOURSELF WITH GIVERS

Raymond impressed the CEO of a large hospital organization with his marketing prowess, and he was given a prestigious role in the company. His opportunity for advancement seemed limitless. Before he started, the CEO and his wife took Raymond and his wife out to dinner.

Throughout the meal, Raymond detected his wife's faint scowl. The other couple didn't seem to notice, but he sure did. As they drove home, he asked, "What in the world was going on with you? I know you saw something. What is it?"

She unloaded on him: "I don't trust the CEO as far as I can throw him!" She pointed out some inconsistencies in the man's stories, and she also explained that he had treated his wife as an afterthought, rarely involving her in the conversation and seldom even glancing in her direction. "And you think you're going to be happy working for him?" she snapped at Raymond. It wasn't a question he wanted to answer. He hoped his wife was wrong, but he couldn't easily dismiss her observations. She had been right about people too often before.

For about a year, everything went really well for Raymond in his new role as VP of marketing, and then the wheels came off. The CEO needed a scapegoat for a failed venture, and he blamed Raymond for the debacle. When Raymond tried to talk about it with him, the CEO exploded in anger. It got worse from there. Raymond fell from his position as the golden boy of the company to being the whipping boy for the CEO. The grind of working in the office with his CEO led to many sleepless nights, upset stomachs, and generalized anxiety. Peace of mind? Gone. Purpose and meaning? Vanished. Trust at work? The good vibes at the beginning were now a distant memory.

Day after day, Raymond came home to discuss the situation with his wife. She had two pieces of advice: "Surround yourself with a few trustworthy people who will pour into your life, and pour yourself out to care for others."

Since Raymond felt like he was losing his mind, he was willing to try anything. He called an old friend, told him the story of his last two years of hell at the company, and asked if they could talk once a week for the foreseeable future. His friend was glad to be a listening ear. Raymond also found a life coach who had experience helping executives in similar situations.

Over the next four months, those two men became the givers Raymond needed so he could make sense of his present and figure out his future. With their support and insight, he no longer felt alone. He developed a plan to resign and find a job in another company.

In the meantime, Raymond realized a number of people in the company were very unhappy with the CEO. He had to be very careful not to lead an insurrection, so he carefully selected a few people to help along in the same way his friend and coach were doing for him. When he saw the difference he could make in their lives just by being a friend, he felt great satisfaction.

Giving frees us from the familiar territory of our own needs by opening our mind to the unexplained worlds occupied by the needs of others.

—Barbara Bush

I can identify with Raymond. When I felt intense stress and discouragement, I went back to the people who had given so much to me during my entire life: my mother and siblings. I told them what was going on and the struggles I was having in trying to cope with the stress. They didn't offer simplistic solutions to complex problems. They listened, cared, and listened some more.

I also sought out a few people who are smarter than me and have been through difficulties at least as difficult as mine. I didn't narrow my search to the insurance industry. I was interested more in the bigger pattern of their life's story: of heartaches healed, torn relationships restored, worry soothed, peace found, and purpose enhanced by the process of healing and hope.

In my darkest times, I've found kind people, honest people, wise people, noble people, and patient people. These people never claimed to be perfect, only to be in the process of growing as human beings.

GRATITUDE AND GIVING

As the tide of my life turned, I realized that generosity provides both relief and joy. When I'm involved in meeting the needs of the homeless and hungry, I realize how bountiful are God's blessings to me. When I care for individuals with health problems, I get a clearer picture of how my health is such as gift. And as I see how my money is helping those in need, I feel real joy that I can make a difference.

But money isn't the main thing I've learned to give. It's perfectly fine to give hundreds or thousands of dollars to any worthy cause, but I've been abundantly blessed by delivering clothing to those who had little. And recently our family, including Lauren, our seven year old, has gone to a soup kitchen to help prepare food for hungry people who can't afford a good meal.

I have to admit that for years I gave money to certain causes, but not my time or my heart. Why? Because I wanted to keep others at arm's length. I didn't like feeling vulnerable around them. But now I know how it feels to be vulnerable, and I want to show love to others who feel lost and alone.

I've made some good strides in this direction, but I need to do more. I want to give more of my time, my heart, and my energy to care for others. I've realized I have a wide network of friends who are professionals, and many of them would be glad to help those in need, pro bono. I'd love to be a switchboard to connect the needy with those generous, gifted people. That's part of my vision for the future.

In every part of my life, I want to complete the circle. My brothers and sisters, my extended family members, my wife and my children are all consummate givers. One of the people who impresses me no end is my brother-in-law, Sharon's husband Mike Jansma. He is a devoted husband, father, and friend. In his business and in his church, people admire him, respect him, and count on him. My mother, Joe Hannah, Jay Green, Jack and Garry Kinder, and many others poured love and life into me when, to be honest, there wasn't a lot to believe in. I'm now pouring more of myself into others, not because they're particularly beautiful or worthy, but because they're human beings, created by God, and of inestimable value.

We have to be honest about our motives. If we serve, give, and care to be noticed and applauded, we're only doing it for ourselves. If, however, we can serve, give, and care without any thought of recognition, we've become true givers.

You can't have a perfect day without doing something for someone who'll never be able to repay you.

—*John Wooden*

THINK ABOUT IT . . .

1. How would you describe the impact of "takers" on our lives? Who have been some takers in your life? How is your life impoverished because of them? Is the sting still there? Explain your answer.

2. How would you describe the influence of "givers"? Who are some people who have played this role in your life? How have they helped you experience peace of mind and a renewed sense of purpose?

3. Describe the four kinds of trust outlined in this chapter: blind, passive, intimidating, and wise. Which of these best represents you? Explain your answer. What steps do you need to take toward wisdom as you try to find and rely on trustworthy people?

4. Do you need some givers to step into your life right now? Where will you find them? How will you ask for their help?

5. What are some ways you can complete the cycle by giving to others?

CHAPTER 6 | **GET REAL**

Far too many people have no idea of what they can do because all they have been told is what they can't do. They don't know what they want because they don't know what's available to them.

—Zig Ziglar

Wishing isn't enough to produce change. Complaining may feel good for the moment, but it often digs the pit of despair a little deeper. Self-pity and passivity aren't the ingredients for a recipe of courage and progress.

Few people, including business leaders, ever conduct a rigorous examination of their companies or their lives. Over time, they create thoroughly familiar patterns of behavior and expectations at work and at home. Unless a calamity rocks their worlds, they drift along on the river of same old same old.

We need to be strong enough and wise enough to get real about our current condition.

TAKE A GOOD LOOK

Our analyses of our present situations, our hopes for the future, and our plans to make progress need to address every part of our lives: our career, our family, our health, and every other important area. Then, after we've evaluated each component, we must be objective about the synergy and balance of all these areas. It's very easy to give too much attention to one part and neglect the rest. Life balance, the beautiful blend of peace and purpose, is achieved only when all of these find their proper place— never perfect, but good and getting better. We'll look at health in the next chapter. For now, we'll focus on two crucial areas: career and family. If you get these right, you'll thrive. If you get them wrong and out of balance, no amount of success can compensate for the pain. Pay attention. This is important.

Career

Early in my career, I developed the habit of regularly evaluating the current state of my business and charting a course to the next stage, always with a much higher vision in mind. One of the most commonly used evaluation methods is SWOT: an analysis of strengths, weaknesses, opportunities, and threats. The business world has hundreds of workable problem-solving methods, and almost all of them will work just fine—as long we actually implement them.

I always start with a detailed profit/loss statement, and I analyze every person and every practice in the company. Who and what are profit centers? Who and what are cost centers? I try to be as objective as possible, but also, I keep in mind that everyone is a learner. Well, that's not really true. All of us *can be* learners. If I suspect an employee has become stagnant and complacent, we'll need to have a talk. Failure, though, isn't the end of the world. We can learn our greatest lessons from failure. But the toxic blend of failure and complacency may be the end of the world— at least as an employee in our office.

In short-term and long-term planning, we need both rigorous realism and a vision of a glorious future—not one or the other, but both. A sweeping vision without clear direction to take the next step is worthless . . . and worse, it's confusing to people in our offices. But narrowly focusing on today's problems and opportunities without a grand plan for growth is boring. It doesn't capture our own hearts, much less the hearts of our employees.

Planning isn't just about taking advantage of opportunities. Several people I've worked with advise those in the planning process to anticipate "the parade of the horribles." They encourage people to consider what might go wrong so they can be ready with contingency plans instead of panicking. For instance, how will the business be affected if the economy goes into a declining phase of a normal economic cycle? Today in the insurance business, we need to consider how we'll respond to the new technology of the driverless car. Some experts predict far fewer claims because there will be less driver error, but others worry about who will be held responsible for any accidents, the driver or the company that developed the technology.

Purpose is the place where your deep gladness meets the world's needs.

—Frederick Buechner

Family

Some of us have lived with low-level tension in our marriages and with our kids for so long that gritting our teeth when we walk through the door of our homes is SOP, standard operating procedure. Many people live in relationships that are little more than an armed truce, and for a few, the truce is regularly broken by outbursts of anger and recriminations.

Healing may happen slowly or quickly, but it can only occur when we have the courage to start the process by owning our part. If trust has been eroded by a million little offenses or shattered by a single big one, it can be restored, slowly and carefully, through sincere words backed by consistent actions.

In some families, the wounds haven't been caused by outbursts of venomous words, but by the painful absence created by someone who values career success over the family. I'm not suggesting that a person in business never call to say she needs to stay late to take care of a customer or a problem in the office. But I'm suggesting the absences shouldn't be too frequent or too lenghty, and when she's home, she should be fully attentive to her family. I believe most spouses and kids don't mind us working hard and missing a few meals or events now and then, but they are deeply hurt when our collective actions convince them they really don't matter to us. That's a problem that needs to be addressed . . . immediately and emphatically.

I have to be honest that this has been a problem for me, and it remains a constant tension in my life. My career as a speaker and consultant takes me away from my family and friends. When I'm gone, I need to stay connected, and when I'm home, I need to be fully present with each person. The issue, though, isn't just about time. I need to do whatever it takes for those I love to be convinced that I treasure them.

Family relationships cause our deepest pains, but they can also bring our greatest joys. Enjoy laughter, tell stories, and invest in activities that cement the bonds of affection. Psychologist Gary Chapman has identified five different ways people give and receive love. He calls them "love languages."[21] Some people appreciate gifts; others value heartfelt words of tenderness and affirmation. Some simply want time together, others thrive on hugs, and some really appreciate efforts that show we care, like washing the dishes without being asked. The point is this: Don't be a dummy. Identify the love language for each person in your family, and tailor your words and actions to communicate love to each one. Don't assume they're just like you. They probably aren't. Become a student of their languages, and become creative and proficient in speaking them. Sure, it takes some effort, but it's worth it. You'll be amazed at the difference it makes.

BALANCE AND FOCUS

Your relationships with friends, your hobbies, and all other interests take a backseat to the central importance of your family and your career. Finding the right balance takes honesty, input from mentors and friends, communication, negotiation, and a large helping of trial and error . . . all of which may prompt many, many midcourse corrections. In other words, don't expect to get everything correct from the beginning. And as life changes—babies, houses, moves, promotions, graduations, marriages, and so on—you'll have to continually adjust to determine the right balance.

I'm a fan of excellence, but inordinate perfectionism and worry steal my attention and erode my energy. I've noticed that I'm not as fully engaged at work if I'm concerned about what's going on at home, and I'm not attentive to my wife and kids if I'm worried about problems at the office. To remain completely focused on the tasks and the people in front of me at every point during the day, I need peace, which comes from a mind uncluttered by conflict and unrelieved stress. Resolving problems at home makes me a better businessman, and being confident at work frees me to be a better husband and father. This observation is intuitively obvious, but sadly, many of us have learned to live with perpetual tension, disappointment, and heartache all day every day. It's become so much a part of our daily lives that we don't notice the damage, and we don't do anything to change it. A world of peace and purpose is available, but many people are either blind or have lost hope that these essentials of life are even possible any longer. Yes, they're possible, but they require honesty, courage, action, and persistence.

———————————— ❖ ————————————

Our greatest fear should not be of failure, but of succeeding at things in life that don't really matter.

—**Francis Chan**

BIG GOALS, SMALL STEPS

I'm a dreamer who values the process of taking incremental steps to achieve my audacious goals. Each of us needs to take time to imagine what life might be like if we accomplish something really big at work and in our families. In our careers, we may imagine starting a business, building an existing business, or playing a pivotal role in an organization. We may assign a numerical target to our vision of the future, or it may still be in the conceptual stage. At some point, as the vision gels, we need to begin to identify the big steps we'll need to take to reach our goal. We need to ask: What are stages of growth and development? What do we need to know, be, and do at each stage? What resources will we need, and when will we need them?

When it comes to our families, what qualities do we want in those relationships? Many people don't have a clue, and need to spend time with strong, creative, healthy families to get a picture of what a family might be. Others only need to think back to the love and laughter they enjoyed as kids. The big vision of a loving family then needs the same kind of stage planning. What are the marks of a great family? What are the stages our family needs to travel to get there? What is each person's love language? How can we carve out enough quantity time so that at least some of it becomes quality time? (I believe it's impossible to have quality time without quantity. We can't say to our teenage daughters, "We're going to be together from 8:00 to 9:00 on Thursday night. Come ready to tell me your highest hopes and deepest fears." Life just doesn't work like that.)

Instead of being exhausted by overwork or passive due to fear of conflict, a healthy family finds creative ways to interact. They try new things, learn new skills, and go new places. Every experience strengthens the growing legacy of love and trust.

Detailed planning isn't a waste of time as some people suspect. They point out that distractions and unforeseen circumstances can get in the way, so what's the use in planning? Good plans, though, aren't a straitjacket; we can always be flexible and responsive to situations and people. Daily and weekly plans can provide clear direction in a chaotic world. I regularly catalog everything I need to do. I may have a hundred things on the list. A few days later, if I analyze the list, I often realize I've done more than half of them. The very act of recording them engraves the items on my mind. Consciously or subconsciously, I'm more focused on the things I've written, and I'm far more likely to accomplish them, which makes me far more effective as a businessman, husband, father, and friend.

GET A GRIP ON TIME

Some people have very clear, carefully constructed plans for their work, and they also have detailed plans for their families, but they fail to synthesize the two planning sheets. Instead of streamlining and complementing each other, the competing plans produce even more tension and anxiety. The instrument that helps us keep the right focus is a calendar. On mine, I put every priority, every meeting, and every to-do item for the day, week, and month. A maxim of my life is that I never start a day until I've completed my daily schedule. With it, I'm a focused warrior; without it, I tend to wander.

On my calendar, I naturally include the confirmed appointments I set up or my assistant sets up for me, but I also write down all the relational, non-confirmed appointments (NCAs) that keep me connected to the people I love. For instance, I put people's birthdays on my calendar, so when I have a short break, I can send five "happy birthday" messages on Facebook. It only takes a few seconds to let others know I'm thinking of them and I value their friendship. But if they weren't on my calendar, there's no way I'd remember their birthdays.

The NCAs aren't incidental or expendable. They're crucial to me and to those I care about. I don't end my day until I've made progress in contacting the people on this list. Of course, some days are more open than others, so I have to remain flexible. Deepak Chopra observed, "You don't want to stand rigid like a tall oak that cracks and collapses in the storm. Instead, you want to be flexible, like a reed that bends with the storm and survives."[22]

I talk to spouses who complain that their husband or wife never carves out time for family vacations. The delinquent spouses often complain that they forgot to schedule it, and work built up so much they can't go. A calendar will fix that problem. I put my family's vacations on my calendar months in advance, and sometimes a full year if it's a special trip. We then have plenty of time to prepare for a great experience, change plans if we find something better, and pay for it when we can get the best deals.

Rich people have twenty-four hours in a day and poor people have twenty-four hours in a day. You have twenty-four hours and I have twenty-four hours. You can't save time; you can only use it effectively.

—*Jim Rohn*

In many ways, my calendar is my life, but it's not a burden in the least. I'm tied to it in a way that gives me more freedom, peace, and confidence than when I'm "winging it." When he was in office, President George W. Bush divided his day into fifteen-minute segments. He was determined to get the most out of each block of time. Before I read about President Bush, I instinctively carved out segments of time to devote to particular purposes—and I still do.

I tell people to "make a date with yourself" by blocking out time to think about an issue or perform a task. When I look at my calendar, I want to maximize every minute of the day. Each fifteen-minute block of time is a "unit." When I conduct an insurance review with a customer, I block out two units. Thirty minutes is plenty of time for me to ask all appropriate questions and listen to the answers. On other days, I might devote twenty units, five hours, to a particular project. In this way, I'm fully aware of how long each encounter or task will take, and I seldom waste time. This doesn't necessarily mean I'm so driven I never rest. Taking breaks and relaxing are part of my schedule, so I put them on my calendar. In this way, I get the most out of life. I believe every minute is precious and meaningful, and I'm certainly flexible enough to change whenever something more important surfaces.

A few years ago, you could buy all kinds of planners at the local office supply shop. You can still use one of those (if you can find them), but you can also find a wealth of scheduling resources online. Talk to your friends to see which ones they recommend, and then dive in to give one a try. If you love it, keep using it. If it doesn't work for you, keep looking until you find one that does.

The vast majority of people spend too much time on some things and too little on others. It's not because they're intellectually challenged; it's because they didn't take a few minutes each day to put their priorities on their calendar. A workable calendar enables us to invest our lives in the things we've said we treasure most, and it provides us plenty of opportunities to make necessary changes so our day reflects our values. A calendar is one of the most important tools to help us find balance and stay balanced. A clear, purpose-driven schedule gives us confidence and peace of mind. Don't start another day without one.

I instinctively combine my calendar with a profit and loss analysis, and I bet you do, too. People who have goals (and that includes almost all of us) are always thinking, always calculating. I simply try to combine three things: the compelling goals in my career and my family, my analysis of success and failure in every area, and my calendar. My goals keep me focused on what's really important in life, my analysis shows me where I'm doing well and where I need to give more attention, and my calendar puts my plans into action at specific points. Does this sound complicated? It's not. When you grasp the connection among the three components, it's very easy and amazingly effective.[23]

This life strategy isn't reserved for the CEO or president of a company. Anyone anywhere can use it, from the top corporate execs to the high school student. Every person probably needs to talk to a few others—wise, mature, successful others—in their field to get feedback on goals, objectives, plans, and a reasonable timeline. Each occupation and each role has its own metrics. For instance, a mid-level manager at a large corporation is probably responsible for ten to twenty employees. Salaries are one of the most significant costs for any company and in any division. The manager needs to often ask, "Is the payroll the right amount for the revenue my department is bringing in?" In insurance and other personal services industries, thirty percent is a good benchmark for salaries to revenues. If it's less than that, the department is running lean and is more profitable. Some managers spend more on salaries during a time when the department is expanding and they're investing in the future. A department may have payroll expenses less than the benchmark but not be profitable because the current roster can't take advantage of all the opportunities. The benchmark is helpful, but the analysis has to take a number of factors into consideration.

The manager then needs to thoroughly assess the productivity of the department and each employee. Today, the corporate world has a vast array of tools to help managers get an accurate reading on productivity, including individuals and teams. With this evaluation, the manager can have a personal development plan for each position. The plan addresses all the stages of employment, including interviewing prospective employees, hiring, onboarding, training, and supervising.

The analysis also includes the manager's skills in communicating with his staff. Do the employees understand the goals of the department? Have they bought in? In other words, has the manager inspired them with a vision of how meeting the goals will bring benefit to them, the department, the company, and especially, the customers?

Part of the overall assessment is a detailed analysis of the processes in the office and in communication with customers and vendors. How are new customers handled? How are claims or complaints addressed? How do the communications lines work within the office? How do you use email, text, social media, phone, and personal meetings to get the job done? Where are things running smoothly? Where are there delays or misunderstandings or dropped balls? Processes are as varied as the products and services companies produce, and even within companies different divisions may have very different cultures.

Sooner or later, the manager will realize others on the team have greater skills in some areas and can make a greater contribution if given the chance. Many years ago, I tried to be all things to all people. I tried very hard, but I felt frustrated and dropped too many balls. I asked my sister Sharon to come on board as my partner, and soon I discovered she is a far better leader than I am or ever will be. She's far superior in sales and service, an outstanding recruiter, and a better trainer and manager. I was barely smart enough to give her an open door and get out of her way to let her do her masterful job.

------------------------ ❖ ------------------------

We must accept finite disappointment, but we must never lose infinite hope.

—Dr. Martin Luther King, Jr.

The mid-level manager also has a family at home, and he needs to be at least as successful there as he is in the office. He knows he can't afford to give his tired hours to his wife and kids and expect them to have emotional tanks that are full and overflowing. Without saying what he's doing, the manager can do a profit/loss analysis for his family. The profit is love, hugs, laughs, kidding, celebrating every success, comforting people when they're down, and encouraging them when they're fearful. To this depth of relationships, they need creative interaction—without cellphones, computers, or videogames, unless, of course, they want to spend some time playing together using these devices. When the manager is under stress, creativity and joy gradually fade, and relating to the spouse and kids becomes a grind . . . or a threat. That's when family experiences significant loss.

Take your kids to the office to let them see the people you work with and how you help the people in your community. When you go home each day, tell them stories about meaningful interactions and victories. Years ago, I sometimes took my kids to the office on Saturday when I cleaned the place. They might pitch in to help, or they played in the conference room, but either way, they had a sense of where their dad spent time each day. Don't dump your frustrations on your kids. You can say you've had a hard day, but they don't need to know the particulars of office politics and how a jerk mistreated you. Give them a positive view of your work, and let them see the value of doing a job with care, excellence, and integrity.

I've lived on both sides. I've invested time and money in great trips with my family, as simply as going to a park near the house to more elaborate and expensive trips that loudly proclaim, "I value you so much that I want to celebrate our family!" But even then, the expenses are always within the budget. For years, we scrimped in certain areas so we could splurge in others. A good budget helps you fulfill your priorities without breaking the bank.

As your children grow, involve them more in dreaming great dreams for the family, setting goals, and making plans. And always make sure to value their payoffs. My older kids love Disneyland, which is in Anaheim, three or four hours south of our community in California. A trip there is a reward for our family. We use a family visit to Disneyland to celebrate anything and everything: moving up a grade in school, passing a test, reaching a business goal for me, and a hundred other things we're excited about.

With these experiences as a background, it's easy to invite our kids to think and dream about the next big wins in the family. They can think of dozens of them! And they're sure that reaching their goals will end in a celebration. For them, goal setting, planning, and scheduling aren't drudgery. They don't dread hours of dull training sessions in a hotel ballroom. They see these management skills as the obvious and essential tools to make life exciting! That's not a bad perspective for any of us.

Like I do in my personal planning and my planning for my business, our family puts our dreams, plans, and schedule on paper. The sheer act of writing clarifies our thinking, forces us to be precise, and affirms our commitment.

GOALS, PLANS, AND VALUES

Wishes are good and wonderful, but they don't change anything until they become plans that are committed to a schedule. Here's the way I see it:

- A person without a vision is a wanderer.

- A vision without a plan is only a dream.

- A plan without a schedule is frustrating and confusing.

- But a person who crafts all of these with heart and skill will see magnificent progress in every area of life.

People can perceive the planning process as cold, dry, and lifeless, but I see it as life giving. The process enables me to get real. My dreams, evaluations, plans, and schedule are essential ingredients to create a life focused on my cherished values, which then gives me peace of mind and reinforces the compelling purpose I want to live for each day. Cold, dry, and lifeless? Not a chance.

One isn't necessarily born with courage, but one is born with potential. Without courage, we cannot practice any other virtue with consistency. We can't be kind, true, merciful, generous, or honest.

—Maya Angelou

THINK ABOUT IT . . .

1. On a scale of 0 (hate to plan, prefer to wing it) to 10 (can't live without my plan and schedule), where are you? How is this working for you?

2. What are some reasons we need both big goals and small steps? What happens when either one is missing?

3. Do you put all of your priorities, responsibilities, and events on a schedule? If so, how does it help you? If not, how might a detailed schedule keep you focused and help you be more successful at home and at work?

4. Which of the principles and suggestion in this chapter do you want (or need) to try? How will it help you?

5. What is the connection between your analysis, planning, and scheduling . . . and achieving peace of mind and fulfilling your purpose in life?

CHAPTER 7

NOT ALL IN YOUR HEAD

If it weren't for the fact that the TV set and the refrigerator are so far apart, some of us wouldn't get any exercise at all.

—*Joey Adams*

I don't run, and I don't do crunches. I've never been on a SEAL team, and no one has asked me to be the star of an exercise video. I walk. That's the only exercise I get, but I absolutely, positively have to carve out time in my schedule to walk regularly or everything in my life deteriorates. When I don't walk, my mind isn't as sharp, but my words often are. That's not a good tradeoff.

Even if I'm not a gym rat who uses every machine and can't feel good until he exerts himself to the point of exhaustion, I still find plenty of excuses to skip today's walk . . . and tomorrow's . . . and the next day's. "It's too early." "It's too late." "I'm too tired." "I have too much to do." "I don't want to get sweaty." "I can schedule an appointment during that time." "I want to relax." "I'm depressed." "It won't do any good." "I'm too stressed out." At various times, all these excuses have crossed my mind. But everything in my life goes better when I consistently walk for forty minutes to an hour each day.

Of my many failures, one of the biggest was not paying attention to my physical health earlier in life. My brothers and sisters were great athletes; I wasn't. My friends were on sports teams in high school, and many of them played for colleges or on club teams at their universities. Some of them became professional athletes in their sports. I was in the choir. The only exercise I got was carrying my books. After I graduated, I tried to make it in the music business. When that didn't work, I was completely devoted to the insurance business. Exercise wasn't even on my radar.

To make things worse, I ate too much. At dinner with my family, I ate everything on my plate. Then I watched like a hawk as my children left half a hamburger or part of their chicken or lasagna, and I swooped in for the kill. By the time dinner was over, all the plates were stacked in front of me. I thought I was being prudent and frugal. After all, who wants to waste food? But I didn't stop there. I often had a big bowl of ice cream late at night before I went to bed.

For years, I daily depleted my physical batteries without recharging them. Only when the deficits became severe did I begin to pay attention to exercise, nutrition, and sleep.

THE PREVENTABLE EPIDEMIC

We've read and heard dire health statistics so often that we don't even pay attention any longer—until we become one of the statistics. My depression was, in equal parts, mental, emotional, relational, spiritual, and physical. Each aspect affects the others. Neglecting my body had significant consequences on the rest of my life. It's small comfort to know I'm not alone.

A report by the President's Council on Fitness, Sports and Nutrition reports:

- Only one in three adults has the recommended level of physical activity each week.

- Children now spend more than seven and a half hours each day in front of some type of screen.

- Less than twenty percent of adults meet the guidelines for aerobic and muscle-strengthening exercise.

- Over forty years, the average daily intake of Americans increased by 600 calories.

- Ninety percent of Americans eat more sodium than recommended, leading to health problems costing about $20 billion a year.

- Empty calories from sugars and fats account for about forty percent of daily calories for children.

- Obesity in children has tripled over a forty-year reporting period, and it doubled for adults.

- Obesity-related sickness, including chronic problems like diabetes and heart disease, disability, and death, costs the economy about $190 billion annually.

- Twenty-seven percent of young people are too overweight to serve in our armed forces.[24]

In a related study on the effects of sleep loss, other statistics come to light:

- Twenty percent of Americans report getting less than six hours of sleep per night.

- An estimated 100,000 car accidents occur each year because drivers are drowsy.

- Depression has been linked to sleep disorders as both a cause and an effect.

- In a Sleep in America survey, twenty-eight percent reported they had missed work or family events, or made errors at work in the past three months due to problems related to lack of sleep.[25]

The only valid excuse for not exercising is paralysis.

—Moira Nordholt

The Centers for Disease Control and Prevention reports, "Chronic diseases and conditions—such as heart disease, stroke, cancer, diabetes, obesity, and arthritis—are among the most common, costly, and preventable of all health problems." These problems are found in almost half of the adult population and are responsible for eighty-four percent of all health care spending in a recent year.[26]

ME, TOO

The startling statistics aren't just about "those other people." Many of us see the damaging impact of poor exercise, nutrition, and sleep when we look at our tired faces in the mirror each morning. I'm not necessarily suggesting we all hire personal coaches to help us get healthy, but that's not a bad idea for many of us. I recommend a common sense approach and a modicum of discipline to take us big steps toward physical health. This is not a negotiable, secondary pursuit. It's essential if we're going to enjoy success and sanity.

If you want to build an insurance business, I'm your guy to follow. If you want to know how to grow virtually any business and manage people effectively, many consider me an expert. When it comes to physical health, I'm only a fellow learner, and a slow one at that—but at least I've learned to stop neglecting this important area of my life. I'm working at it, and I still have a lot to learn.

Modern culture is hectic and distracting. Only a few generations ago, most people lived on farms. With the strenuous labor required, getting adequate exercise wasn't a problem. In the years before electricity, which became more accessible in much of the country only in the 1930s, people often went to bed right after the sun went down and got up before it rose the next morning. Even in the summers, they got plenty of sleep. Some had trouble getting enough to eat when the harvest was lean, but most families grew their own food and had enough.

Today, we're wired, we're mobile, and we're busy. We've invented a million devices to make life easier, and they have been exceedingly successful. The promise was that the inventions would make life simpler and easier, but our lives have become far more complex. We have to make dozens of decisions every morning before we go to work, and we make hundreds more during the day and when we get home. Modern life certainly isn't simple. It's demanding and complicated, which raises our stress levels and threatens to deplete our meager reserves. We sleep less and eat more of the wrong things because we don't have time to cook. And exercise can easily become a low priority. Yet if we don't stop to take care of our bodies, minds, and hearts, we soon are running on fumes. Even relaxing doesn't recharge our engines. We bark at people for the slightest perceived offense, and we don't enjoy much of anything.

This is a description of my life a few years ago. I lived that way so long that I didn't even know another way existed. Even worse, I began to think of rabid busyness and exhaustion as badges of honor. That was so dumb.

Before I came to my revelation that life could be different, I found diversions from the chaos of my life in television shows. In the early years,

Jay Green—the Farmers district manager who originally hired me—sometimes called my home to ask why I was AWOL. I said, "Do you really want to know?"

He laughed as he said, "Yeah, I do."

I answered, "I'm watching *Gilligan's Island.*"

I'm sure Jay shook his head and smiled as he told me, "Troy, come on back. He's not getting off the island."

I've escaped the hectic nature of my life by watching plenty of shows over the years, from *The Brady Bunch* years ago to, more recently, *Law and Order* and *Modern Family*. I've sat in front of the screen watching episodes I'd seen ten times before. I could quote the lines as well as the actors did, but those programs let me escape for a while.

I believe that the Good Lord gave us a finite number of heartbeats and I'm damned if I'm going to use up mine running up and down a street.

—Neil Armstrong on jogging, in an interview with Walter Cronkite

I eventually discovered I needed more than escape; I needed to address the root cause of the problem. Exercise is an important piece of the puzzle. When I go for a good walk and get my heart rate up, my mind clears. I'm not checking email, and I'm not reviewing business plans. I get away to enjoy nature, think and pray, or maybe talk to someone. When I walk, I'm not distracted by all the other demands of my day. If I'm walking with someone or talking on the phone, I can be fully there with the person.

I wish I played golf. When I hear others talk about their time on the course, I can't help but be a little envious. They have about four hours to relax and be together. They're not marketing and they're not selling, but at some point one of the foursome will usually ask, "How are things in your business?" In that context, talking about work is natural and unforced, and others have time to listen and comment. Quite often, such casual conversation leads to a question about the person's insurance needs (or whatever business the players happen to be in).

I do my best to walk every morning. If I could, I'd walk every day in the Sierra Mountains near my cabin at Shaver Lake. The scenery is breath-taking, and you never know what you'll see around the next switchback or curve in the trail. It might be a meadow blanketed with wildflowers, a deer, or a scene of snow-covered peaks that's stunning in the sunlight. Of course, in California, you might also have a mountain lion watching you, a reality that adds a bit of drama to the hike!

Exercise releases endorphins, which fuel happiness and optimism. When I was depressed, my endorphins were missing in action. I needed a kick-start to release them into my brain, but instead, I avoided exercise like it was the Black Plague. The spiral downward continued for far too long. When my brother Alan saw me, he didn't try to be diplomatic, and he didn't mince words. He looked me in the eye and said, "Troy, I can tell you're depressed. You need to get up and get some exercise. It'll make you feel better." He was absolutely right. In my blue funk, I was more resistant than ever to take steps to exercise, eat right, and get good sleep, but with his encouragement and the urging of other good friends, I manned up and started to make better decisions each day. It made all the difference in the world in my outlook. Gradually, hope returned.

Of course, we can all think of a dozen excuses (or at least one com-pelling one) to give up, to remain passive, and to stay in a funk. Too much alcohol or drugs may have robbed us of energy and self-respect, being overweight may make exercise painful, or we may have filled our schedules with so many meaningless activities that we insist, "I'm too busy." Don't buy your own excuses. Do whatever it takes to move forward. Your life, the people you love, and your legacy depend on your digging deep to find the courage to take these steps.

An hour of basketball feels like 15 minutes. An hour on a treadmill feels like a weekend in traffic school.

—David Walters

FALL AND REBOUND

The board of a major technology firm tapped Stanley to be the next CEO. The company had been in shambles for a couple years. Mismanagement and a series of failed products had caused the stock price to plummet. Stanley had been the VP of production, so he knew the business, but no one knew if he could turn the ship around. In the first year, Stanley proved to be a brilliant choice. He handled discord on the board with a blend of diplomacy and power. In addition, he replaced a number of top executives in the company. Stanley was making dramatic moves—it was obvious he was going to be a spectacular success or a colossal failure.

When he became the CEO, Stanley already had some innovative products in the pipeline, but they hadn't gone anywhere . . . until he became the boss. Soon after he took over, he gave the green light to production. A brilliant marketing plan soon followed. Some of the board members thought he was moving too fast, and a few of his top VPs secretly plotted a coup to take advantage of the failure they were sure was coming.

Instead, they were shocked by the success. Stanley astutely anticipated market trends and launched two new products that were instant hits with customers. The stock price soared. A couple of week later, Stanley was featured on the cover of three major business magazines. He could have asked the board to double his salary. Stanley was the biggest star on the biggest stage in his industry.

A week after his face graced the cover of the magazines, a woman on the board sent him an email. She thought she should have been named CEO instead of him, and the recent bulge in her stock portfolio hadn't changed her opinion. She was still jealous and out for blood. Her message was simple, clear, and threatening: "I'm going to take you down!"

Stanley should have had all the confidence in the world, but he wondered what she might bring up that would embarrass him. Did she really have information that would torpedo his reputation and his role?

The next few days, Stanley canceled all his appointments and paced in his office. In his troubled mind, he imagined dozens of scenarios, all of them ending in the destruction of his career. Others in his office were jubilant over the company's recent successes, but Stanley's mood only darkened. A week of sleepless nights and haunted days drove him to the breaking point. In the middle of the day, he mumbled to his executive assistant that he was going out for a while. She asked when he planned to be back, but he didn't answer.

Stanley drove fifty miles to his family's beach house, where he collapsed—mentally, emotionally, and physically. For two days, no one, even his family, knew where he was. Then his wife Anna put some pieces together. She couldn't help but notice his declining condition. After she couldn't reach him on any device, she drove to the beach house to see if he was hiding there.

When Anna walked in and called his name, Stanley wasn't sure if he felt more relieved or ashamed. She found him in the bedroom, and they embraced. She didn't ask any questions, and she didn't berate him for worrying her to death during the two days of silence. After their hug, she smiled at him, whispered for him to lie back down on the bed, and went to get the groceries she had brought, anticipating his condition. She carefully prepared one of his favorite dishes: spicy chicken cacciatore with a Caesar salad.

After an hour or so in the kitchen, Anna brought the elegantly plated meal to the bedroom. Stanley sat up and devoured the dish like it was the first thing he'd eaten in days—because it was. When he finished, Anna took the plate away and said only, "I think it would be good to get some sleep." She kissed him on the forehead and left the room.

Stanley slept for thirteen hours. When he woke up, he felt like at least part of the world had been lifted from his shoulders. Anna was waiting for him in the living room. She had her athletic shoes on, and she said, "I'll cook you a nice breakfast, and then we can go for a walk."

Stanley smiled and said softly, "Great."

Anna prepared an omelet with an English muffin. Stanley ate and had two cups of coffee. Neither of them said a word, but they both understood that a dam was breaking in his mind and heart. Stanley went back into the bedroom, found some shorts and a pair of hiking shoes in the closet, and put them on.

The two of them walked down the long stairs to the sand dunes, then through a passage between the dunes to the beach. They walked for two hours, rarely saying a word. When they got back to the house, Stanley poured out his fears to Anna. She listened tenderly without giving advice. Finally, she reached over and touched his hand. She looked into his eyes and said softly, "Stanley, you're the best man I've ever known. You're a gifted executive and a brilliant leader, but more than that, you're a wonderful person. I love you so much."

Stanley called his office to tell them he'd be back in a couple of days. He told his executive assistant to tell anyone who asked that he simply had needed a break, and he apologized for not letting them know sooner he would be gone for a while.

When he returned to his office, Stanley had more confidence than ever, but he was never cocky again. The days of darkness had taught him that no one is impervious to threats, even supremely successful people. In fact, successful people are sometimes more vulnerable because they don't see the threats coming. Stanley would never be naïve again.

It wasn't until my late twenties that I learned that by working out I had given myself a great gift. I learned that nothing good comes without work and a certain amount of pain. When I finish a set that leaves me shaking, I know more about myself. When something gets bad, I know it can't be as bad as that workout.

—Henry Rollins

Does this story sound vaguely familiar? It should if you've read the history of ancient Israel in the Bible. The same storyline occurred in the life of Elijah.[27] He was fantastically successful as a leader of God's people. He came to the forefront during a time of chaos and corruption, and he pointed the people in the right direction. His career was marked by one of the most awesome acts of God found in the Scriptures: calling down the fire of God on Mount Carmel to prove that God is far greater than any other god. But immediately following this stunning success, the threat of one woman, Queen Jezebel, sent him into a tailspin of despair, exhaustion, and physical collapse.

When Elijah had lost all hope, God didn't yell at him, "Just get over it!" Instead, when Elijah was so depressed that he wanted to die, God gave him sleep, good food, more sleep, another great meal, and then sent him on a long hike. Only after this process of physical and mental restoration, God spoke to him to give him directions. Even then, God didn't communicate through a mighty wind, an earthquake, or a raging fire. God spoke to Elijah in a gentle whisper to remind him of His love and purpose for his life.

Please don't misunderstand me. Many times people need professional therapeutic help and medications to help them get out of depression. The medications raise a person's emotional floor so she doesn't sink so deep into despair, and they help clear the mind so she can think more clearly about the past, the present, and the future. But we shouldn't neglect the restorative processes already present in the human body. The lack of exercise, good food, and sleep may not be the most significant cause of a person's depression or physical disease, but they certainly exacerbate the problems related to stress. In the life of Elijah and the life of every one of us, adequate exercise, good nutrition, and enough sleep are essential in the good times to keep us healthy and sane, and they are equally important when we suffer from the discouragement and losses of life and we feel like the world is against us.

You don't have to use a Marine's workout schedule and diet to make progress. You only need to do some simple, reasonable things to get started. But you need to start.

I'll never run, and you won't ever find me on the floor doing crunches. But I walk, I try to eat healthy foods in healthy portions, and I turn off the lights at a reasonable hour so I can get enough sleep. These steps are the least I can do, and they are the least you can do, too.

Take the first step, and your mind will mobilize all its forces to your aid. But the first essential is that you begin. Once the battle is startled, all that is within and without you will come to your assistance.

—Robert Collier

THINK ABOUT IT . . .

1. What is a time in your life when you've been the healthiest? What were you doing with exercise, food, and sleep?

2. When you've struggled with down times, what were you doing about exercise, food, and sleep?

3. What are the most common excuses you've heard about why people don't take care of themselves in these three areas? Which excuses have you used . . . this week?

4. How would you describe the restorative powers of the body when a person has crashed under intense stress? How much sleep, good food, rest, and exercise does a person need to recover? When does a person need to seek professional help?

5. What is your reasonable plan to take steps in these areas? What do you need to *stop* doing, what do you need to *start* doing, and what do you need to *keep* doing?

    —Exercise

    Stop doing:

    Start doing:

    Keep doing:

    —Healthy eating

    Stop doing:

    Start doing:

    Keep doing:

    —Getting enough sleep

    Stop doing:

    Start doing:

    Keep doing:

| # BIG ROCKS FIRST

The key is not to prioritize what's on your schedule, but to schedule your priorities.

— Stephen Covey

I've always been a disciplined person, but I haven't always been a smart person. Wisdom comes from experience, and even then, we gain wisdom only if we pay attention to our experiences and make necessary changes. For years, everything in my life seemed equally important. More accurately, they seemed equally *urgent*. I had to get them all done, and all done right now!

I heard an analogy years ago that instantly made perfect sense. You have a box, which represents the time allotted to you each day. You also have a bunch of rocks—big ones, little pebbles, and all sizes in between. These represent our priorities, from the most important to the not-so-important, and there are more rocks than will easily fit in the box. If you randomly grab the ones closest to you and throw them into the box, you'll probably fill it up with small and medium-sized rocks, leaving no room for some of the larger ones. If, however, you start with the big rocks, follow with the medium-sized ones, and then fill in as many little ones as will fit, you'll get far more into the box. If any are left outside, they are the smallest ones.

When I heard this analogy, I realized I'd been grabbing every pebble and stone within reach every moment of every day, and my box was often too full for the really important things in my life. I was busy, I was diligent, and I was working like a madman, but my biggest priorities were being neglected—not from laziness, but because I didn't understand the principle of priorities.

This concept was reinforced by the Kinder brothers, Jack and Garry. They analyzed the pursuit of goals as "minimum" standards and "superior" performance.[28] When we set our goals low, our priorities don't matter that much. We can probably meet the minimum standard—often set by the company, our boss, or our spouse and kids—without having to think very hard about what matters most. But if we want to achieve a superior status, we have to rigorously set and adhere to priorities. Establishing priorities forces us to distinguish between the *urgent* things screaming for our attention right now and the *important* matters that promise real progress and success.

I quickly realized that one of my top priorities was to find people to join me so I'd be free to focus on what I do best. But they had to be the right people. My sister Sharon has proven to be an incredibly valuable asset to our team and to me. She has management skills I'll never have. My role is to assist her with the vision and strategy . . . and then get out of her way. We talk all the time about specific customers, goals, employees, and strategies, and I trust her implicitly. The rest of our team has changed over the years, but the same principle is true: our priority is to have a highly skilled, top performing team so that we provide outstanding service to our customers.

Part of the strategy to live by priorities is to schedule particular tasks at the right time of the day. For me, exercise works best early in the morning. It gets me off to a great start, invigorates my mind, and gives me energy to tackle the day. I often schedule a few minutes at the end of the day to call people to just tell them I'm thinking about them. If they don't answer, I leave a quick message. People appreciate the thought. I know I sure do.

We don't drift in good directions. We discipline and prioritize ourselves there.

—Andy Stanley

CASCADING PRIORITIES

In any organization or family, priorities need to come from the people in authority, or at least, ours need to mesh with the priorities of others. In a company, each employee receives priorities from the level above him. I worked with the president of an outstanding company. One of the traits that made him such a great leader is that he developed a system for crafting and communicating priorities for his business. In a company with 30,000 employees, he worked with his executives to establish the top priorities for the entire company. Then, each department head would take responsibility for the ones that related to that department. The department head would then assign particular priorities to each of the managers, and they made a commitment to communicate often and clearly so that all the priorities of the department were met. The priorities led to detailed plans, specific delegation, and targeted deadlines. Each of the middle managers then used the same procedure with each team in the department. In this way, the president's vision, goals, and priorities cascaded down so that all of the 30,000 employees knew their roles—and all of them were crucial in accomplishing the objectives of the company.

At regular intervals, the president, division VPs, department managers, and team leaders evaluate progress and set intermediate "milestones" to measure incremental progress toward each priority. Hitting the milestones gives people a sense of accomplishment and builds camaraderie. When they miss a milestone, they can evaluate the problem, make necessary adjustments, and keep moving forward. Regularly scheduled analysis doesn't have to be threatening. In fact, it can focus on celebration and affirmation, with tweaks to be sure the team stays on target.

Nothing is less productive than to make more efficient what should not be done at all.

—Peter Drucker

I learned a lot from this brilliant leader, and I've adopted his method in our business. Our list of employees isn't as long as his, but we use the same principles. Sharon and I set our priorities, and then we communicate them to our staff, assigning each one particular goals, developing specific plans, and giving clear deadlines. But these aren't just communicated once with a hope and a prayer they'll be accomplished. Sharon and I consistently review our priorities and the progress we've made during the week. Our analysis lets us fine-tune our plans for the coming week so we can communicate clearly with each person on our team. It works beautifully.

Of course, priorities can change in different ways. If we discover they're too high, too low, or not exactly right in any way, we alter them. And when we fulfill a priority, we move to the next one. Quite often, though, the next one is just a higher goal in the same part of the business. We want to always work on achievable and sustainable priorities, goals that are clear and inspiring.

Most companies have a set of open-ended priorities, ones that are always on the list, such as recruiting, onboarding new employees, training, and supervising. Especially in larger companies, investing in people is always a top priority. But other goals have an end date: a product is produced and launched, a marketing campaign begins and ends, or a building is designed and built. A number of software innovations are designed to help us keep our priorities straight and in front of us. Google Sheets is one I recommend.

PRIORITIES AT HOME

In a marriage, the husband and wife often have many similar goals and desires, but there are always a few friction points. (I ought to know.) Many couples try to deal with problems by not dealing with them at all, which inevitably leads to far worse friction in the future. Instead, they are wise to address their differences, reason with each other, enter into each other's emotional world (notice, both reason and feelings are important), and then negotiate a solution they can both get behind. When they agree, they can communicate their priorities with their kids and get their feedback. It's a huge mistake for one of the parents to communicate his or her treasured goals with the kids before the spouse has agreed. This produces secret alliances or outright preference, which are poison to a family.

Many people put their families on autopilot, and they assume that kids growing up and leaving home is enough of a priority. We can do better than that. Just as we think, plan, and dream about business success, we can think, plan, and dream about building a strong, loving, laugh-filled, meaningful family, with rich conversations, authentic love, and deep trust in one another. That kind of family doesn't just happen. It takes intentional thought, communication, understanding, and prayer—and a large dose of planning and execution to pull off every element. Actually, the same process of setting and fulfilling business priorities can be implemented in the home . . . without the ties and briefcases, of course.

Things which matter most must never be at the mercy of things which matter least.

— *Johann Wolfgang von Goethe*

Priorities in business and home life are seldom static. I often have to recalibrate in both areas. At work, I may realize my goals were too low, or perhaps I shot too high and frustrated our team instead of inspiring them. At home, as kids grow up, their needs change at each stage of development, so my priorities must shift to meet those needs. My investments of time, attention, wisdom, and equipping them with life skills are far different for a teenager going off to college than for a five year old.

At times I have been so focused on business that I didn't adequately plan with my family. They don't need elaborate vision statements and spreadsheets to have a sense that I care about them and we're headed somewhere as a family, but they need to know I'm thinking of how to create the best possible environment for their happiness and growth. A little planning goes a long, long way.

As a part of this planning process, I begin with questions, not statements. Even when my kids were little, I asked them where they wanted to go on vacations, what they wanted for dinner, their opinions on things going on at school and in our community, and all kinds of things to show them I value their desires and perspectives. Disagreements and disappointments are inevitable, whether you set goals or not. Good, open communication, coupled with the desire to live by priorities, gives everyone more security, which is the necessary atmosphere for each person in the family to experience peace and pursue a greater sense of purpose.

One of the most meaningful priorities in a family is caring for others in tangible ways—to be givers instead of takers. I've mentioned our involvement with a local organization providing meals for the poor in our community. A week or so before a recent Christmas, my wife Janette contacted the soup kitchen, and our family went there to prepare dinner. They regularly serve about 250 people. When we walked in, we met the manager and announced, "We're here to help."

He answered, "Great." He pointed to the industrial refrigerators on the far wall and said, "The food is in there, and the grills are over here. It's all yours."

I asked, "What's on the menu for tonight?"

He smiled, "Whatever you find in the refrigerators and freezer." After a pause, he reminded us, "You're cooking for 250, so be sure you fix enough."

That was his complete introduction to menu planning and the intricacies of the kitchen, and that was the entire training program. We rolled up our sleeves, put on aprons, and had the time of our lives deciding what to cook, how to cook it, and how to make it special for the men and women, boys and girls who would show up for dinner that night. Our family will never forget the experience, and we all want to do it again and again. Generosity is contagious.

The mystery of human existence lies not in just staying alive, but in finding something to live for.

— **Fyodor Dostoyevsky**

For a family, the principles of prioritizing are similar to what we do in the business world, but the process is far different. It's more relaxed, more

conversational, and more flexible . . . but just as powerful in drawing people together and infusing meaning into everything we do.

To get away from distractions, take a picnic to the park, go for a drive
into the mountains, walk on the beach, or go out to dinner—no phones,
no video games, and no other devices. You can invite the family by saying
something simple like, "Let's go somewhere so we can talk about what
we want to do this year." When you arrive, enjoy the time together. Ask
questions, but not ones with an edge that actually communicate, "I've got
a plan, and you'd better get on board!" Let people disagree. In fact, value disagreement. (It may blow their minds!) The goal isn't to manipulate
people to come up with what you want, but for everyone to walk away
feeling validated. Ernest Hemmingway remarked, "When people talk, listen completely. Most people never listen."[29]

I suggest asking a few very simple questions:

- "What are we doing as a family that we all value—activities that we
  enjoy and that encourage us to communicate with each other?"

- "What do we want to do that we aren't doing now?"

- "What do we want to have that we don't have right now?"

- "What are some ways we can have a positive influence on others
  who are in need?"

- "How do you want to celebrate our family?"

Quite often, people have widely ranging answers to these questions.
Let them talk, and don't cut them off—unless they simply won't stop
talking, and then interrupt graciously to explain that you want everyone
to give input. Let the brainstorming be open and free flowing. Then you
might say, "Those are great ideas. Let's figure out which ones we want to
focus on now, and maybe which ones we can do later." This opens the

dialogue to establish priorities. You don't need to use the vocabulary you use at the office when you're setting priorities and crafting plans and a schedule with your family, but the principles are the same. Keep the dialogue moving, and make sure everyone feels heard, understood, and valued. The conversation may be so open that you don't complete the plans at the first sitting. That's perfectly fine. The process is more important than finalizing the plan. If people have enjoyed talking and dreaming, they'll be happy to get together again, maybe soon around the dinner table instead of in the mountains or at the beach. Just like your office team, if everyone in the family feels heard, they'll be more likely to give creative ideas and compromise to find workable solutions. Eventually, you'll have clear priorities and a plan to achieve them.

Happiness is not an accident. Nor is it something you wish for. Happiness is something you design.

—Jim Rohn

But the plans don't have to come from you. Volunteering at the soup kitchen wasn't my idea, but when Janette suggested it, I was all in. It was one of the most memorable days in the life of our family, and I wouldn't trade it for the world. But I have to remember that the amazing event happened because someone in our family—not me—had an idea that became a vision that became a plan that got on the schedule and became a treasured experience of serving others. In fact, our shared joy of working together at the soup kitchen before Christmas was so meaningful that we've gone back several times during the year. As always, the experiences have been deeper and richer for some than others, but all of us have been touched.

The environment you choose can stimulate or stifle interaction. I think it's helpful to get away, if only for a few hours and only a few miles. Our home in California is two hours from one of the biggest stands of Giant Sequoias. The General Sherman and General Grant trees are in this forest. A relative called me one day and said, "Troy, why don't you call your family? Let's go have lunch in Grant's Grove."

As always, I had a long list of things on my to-do sheet that day, so I tried to convince him to meet me at a restaurant near my office. He wouldn't have it. "Come on," he insisted. "It'll do you good. We'll grab sandwiches for everybody and enjoy being in the mountain air among those trees."

It was a fantastic day. I loved being with all of them, and I especially appreciated being in that setting. It dawned on me that people come from all over the world to experience the majesty of the enormous trees, but I had begun to take them for granted. What did it cost me to have a shared experience in a fabulous setting? Only a few hours and a few dollars for gas and lunch. Together, we had a wonderful conversation about life, our shared past, and our hopes for the future. It all began with a phone call that interrupted my day.

You and your family may not live near the Sierras and the Sequoias, but most of us live near some kind of setting that stimulates the senses— even if it's a local park. Go there, look and marvel, and let the scenery spark creativity in your dreams and plans.

All plans are works in progress. Review the old ones; keep the good and replace the ones that aren't working very well. Evaluate the use of money, time, interests, responsibilities, relationships with friends and relatives, and everything else that may be priorities for the family.

That's been one of my mantras—focus and simplicity. Simple can be harder than complex: You have to work hard to get your thinking clean to make it simple. But it's worth it in the end because once you get there, you can move mountains.

—Steve Jobs

Let's be honest. Many people dread the kind of interaction I'm suggesting because the family has too much baggage. Emotional gashes from past hurts have never healed, probably because they've never even been addressed. As you think about having this kind of meeting with your family, you might be tempted to open with the remark, "Our first priority is to talk about the obvious tension among us." If you have a Ph.D. or a Psy.D. in psychology, you're equipped to dive into deep waters at the outset. The rest of us need to be far more diplomatic. In fact, if a family is experiencing tension, the first statement by at least one of the parents should be to own his or her part of the responsibility, without pointing any fingers at anyone else. The parent may say, "Hey, I know some of you don't even want to be here, and I understand that. But I want to begin by apologizing for (spell out the wrong). I'm so sorry. Please forgive me."

If the only thing that happens in this conversation is a sincere apology and a request for forgiveness, it will still be a monumental turning point in the family's life. Others may or may not own their part in the family drama. That's fine. It may take some time for them to feel safe enough to admit the hurt they've caused.

Does it seem like a bridge too far to admit wrong to the people you love? It shouldn't be. We're all deeply flawed and innately selfish—certainly me, and undoubtedly you. The three words that do the most to build strong relationships may not be "I love you," but "I was wrong." Try it. You'll be amazed at how it opens conversation, begins to dissolve fears, heals hurts, and starts to rebuild trust.

Human relationships, especially in families, are both art and science. We may know the right thing to say and do, but the complexity of the past and present don't guarantee a particular outcome. For instance, some people refuse to apologize, even when everybody is painfully aware of the offenses. Others may apologize multiple times, but there's no change in behavior, so the repeated words are hollow. Apologies are an open door to far more conversations and reconciliation, not the end of the line. Forgiveness is a beautiful thing, but sadly, too rare. Restoring trust requires honesty, persistence, and consistency—and a fair share of humility. We pay a price to admit our part in the problem, but we pay a far higher price if we hang onto our pride and resistance. There is no higher priority for a family than learning to truly love one another, and forgiveness is always a component of genuine love.

Sometimes when you're overwhelmed by a situation—when you're in the darkest of darkness—that's when your priorities are reordered.

—Phoebe Snow

Ironically, I've noticed that a lot of people who are incredibly gifted and effective in their careers are less than effective when they walk through the doors of their homes. But I also know someone who is equally as successful with her husband and kids as she is with her clients . . . my sister Sharon. I asked her how she does it. Here's what she told me:

I look to the Bible for instruction to give me direction for every aspect of my life. Men like David were powerful warriors and great kings, but they sometimes weren't the best role models in their homes. Others, like Boaz, were both strong and kind. And of course, Jesus is the supreme example of a leader who took time to understand, care for the hurting, and sacrifice himself—in the ultimate way—for others. Though the ancient world was a patriarchal culture, we also find women who blended strength and kindness, boldness and love. The woman described in Proverbs 31 inspires me. She was a very astute businesswoman, but she didn't neglect her family. She honored her husband (who obviously wasn't threatened by her success) and cherished her children . . . and she was beautifully dressed! She's a person I admire and try to emulate.

A balanced life, I discovered very early in my career, doesn't happen by accident. I have to be intentional about developing each area, or at least one or two priorities will suffer from neglect. My first priority is my spiritual life. If I draw deeply on the resources of God's love, wisdom and strength, I'm more effective—and more at peace—in every other area of life. I have to work hard to devote my heart, my time, and my talents to my family and my career, without letting either one get crowded out by the inevitable pressures of life. But I also need to stimulate my mind and keep my body fit.

To make sure all of these function as a cohesive whole, I plan my month, my week, and my day. Distractions and interruptions inevitably come, so I have to be flexible, but I try to avoid losing sight of my priorities. Just like a Stealth bomber needs a computer to guide it to the target—and the computer constantly adjusts the flight according to wind drift, storms, and threats from enemies—my planning process keeps me headed in the right direction and enables me to make countless midcourse corrections.

One of the most important concepts that helps me live a balanced, meaningful, happy life is compartmentalization. I've seen the damage caused when people bring their work worries home, and I've seen what happens when they bring their family struggles to the office. When that happens, they never feel at peace, and they are seldom effective either place. When I'm at work, I try to be completely devoted to the people and tasks at hand. And when I'm at home, I leave the concerns of the office at the door.

Over the years, I've had to learn these lessons many times. It's easy to let priorities slip. But I've also seen the incredible benefits of planning and pursuing a balanced life. It takes effort, but it's well worth it.

WRONG ROCKS

I've made some really boneheaded decisions. I either had wrong priorities, I had them out of place, or I simply didn't put enough emphasis on them. Here are some of the times when I put the wrong rocks into my box at the wrong time.

- I spent far too much money on houses, cars, televisions, and other stuff. I wanted to impress people, but that's a terrible priority. Even if we have the means to buy nice things, we need to look at our underlying motives for spending.

- Similarly, I gave far too much to my kids instead of letting them experience the challenge and the joy of earning, budgeting, and making wise purchases on their own. I thought I was helping them. I wasn't.

- I made business success my ultimate priority, and I neglected the rest of the people and activities in my life.

- I've made some really bad investments. I've had a knack of picking stocks just before the companies cratered—AIG, Countrywide, and MCI are the most notable on my infamous list. My priority was making a killing, not protecting my investments, so I didn't ask enough questions.

- I've endorsed some products without lifting the lid all the way to see what was underneath. In some cases, I later discovered the owners of the companies were unscrupulous. My priority had been making a big splash instead of protecting my reputation.

- Speed was sometimes a higher priority in hiring than character and competence. This always—always—resulted in lingering headaches.

Nobody's life is ever all balanced. It's a conscious decision to choose your priorities every day.

—Elisabeth Hasselbeck

RIGHT ROCKS

I've learned a few lessons over the years. Largely through trial and error (mostly error), I discovered right priorities so I put more big rocks in the box before cramming it with little ones.

- I've listened to my family when they've had dreams, and I've helped them set priorities and fulfill their goals.

- I began giving far more things away. At one point, I looked in my closet and realized I had more shoes, suits, shirts, and other clothes than I'd ever wear. I thought I had a good reason to buy so many pairs of shoes. I wanted enough of the right color and style at each of our houses, so I kept buying them. Soon, visitors marveled at how many pairs I had—and I felt proud that they marveled. Some even took pictures of my closet. It was the lure of impressing people again. But I decided to do a massive clear out. I boxed up shoes, suits, shirts, and ties, and had a young man take them to a local Goodwill receiving location.

- One of my priorities is to "fail fast" and learn lessons quickly so I don't repeat dumb mistakes. Denying the reality of my stupidity is never a good solution. The courage to face facts early prevents more unwise decisions down the road. This is a worthwhile and productive priority in my life.

- I don't endorse any products or services unless I've asked all the right questions, I use them, and I trust the integrity of the owner.

- I've set priorities to fill my mind and heart with insightful messages, take care of my body with exercise, nutrition, and sleep, and spend time with the people I love.

- I've learned to hire slowly and ask the right questions. One of the greatest blessings of my life is that our team works so well together. Some of them are family, and all of them have become trusted friends.

WORTH IT

In business and family life, people fall all along the spectrum from detailed to spontaneous, or from focused to confused. No matter where you are on the continuum today, take steps to dream big dreams and clarify your priorities. Make sure you start with the big rocks. Know what really matters, and make sure you invest plenty of time and attention in those people and activities.

Don't see your priorities as only a one-way street to make your life better. I've discovered that the joy of life is in giving, helping, and serving others. By almost every standard, I've been successful my entire life, but I've only experienced peace of mind and a deep sense of joy as I've focused more on giving to others—giving my time, my resources, and my heart to them. This has become my biggest rock.

——————————————— ❖ ———————————————

No one has ever become poor by giving.

—Anne Frank

THINK ABOUT IT . . .

1. What are some signs a person has misplaced priorities?

2. What are some signs a person has right priorities?

3. In your life, what are (or should be):
    —the big rocks?
    —the medium-sized rocks?
    —the pebbles?

4. What is in the right place in your box right now at work and at home? What needs some adjustments in both areas?

5. As you read the section of the chapter on having conversations with your family to set priorities, what is attractive to you? What seems threatening or unworkable? What are you going to do to create those conversations?

| # THE BIGGEST LESSONS IN LIFE

When we give ourselves permission to fail, we, at the same time, give ourselves permission to excel.

—Eloise Ristad

Some of life's pains are self-inflicted; we could have avoided the hurt and disappointment if we'd made better choices. But other painful events are unavoidable. They may result from natural disasters, unforeseen circumstances in business, or personal betrayal that hit us like a meteor falling out of a clear blue sky. Whatever the source, we can learn life's richest lessons from our most difficult moments—but only if we have the courage to ask the hard questions and go where the answers take us. Excuses never lead to insight, and denial doesn't produce wisdom.

My deepest heartaches are the result of losses suffered in failed and broken relationships. My father's death was a tragic, alcohol-caused accident, and it left a hole in my life. Thanks to my mother, the hole was filled with her attention, care, and wisdom. A few people I've loved and trusted have hurt me deeply. I'm sure they had reasons that seemed to make sense to them, and maybe I contributed to the heartache more than I want to admit, but the wound was open and bleeding in each case. Each time, I felt devastated and confused.

I've noticed that people tend to either overreact or underreact to the difficulties they confront. Even when faced with relatively minor problems, some people immediately jump to catastrophic conclusions and assume the world is coming to an end. They may be gripped by rage, fear, or anxiety, and their emotions cloud their ability to think clearly about what's happening. The people on the other end of the spectrum are also gripped by anger, fear, or anxiety, but their reaction is the polar opposite. Instead of bursting into frantic energy and letting their minds run wild, they shut down emotionally, mentally, and physically. It's like they've decided to crawl into a hole to find safety. At both ends of the spectrum, people have lost perspective on reality, and they've lost the opportunity to find something good in the situation.

Don't be afraid to fail. Don't waste energy trying to cover up failure. Learn from your failures and go on to the next challenge. It's okay to fail. If you're not failing, you're not growing.

—H. Stanley Judd

STAY COOL

Like millions of others who watched the unfolding events in New York on September 11, 2001, my sister Sharon was impressed with the character and behavior of the mayor of New York, Rudy Giuliani. From the moment the planes hit the towers, the mayor was out in the streets among the people. Almost hourly, he spoke words of comfort and hope to the people of his city and the world. He calmly explained what was being done and what couldn't be done. Through it all, he exhibited a trait Sharon dubbed "Rudy Giuliani cool."

That's the kind of response I want to have in any crisis. My tendency is to overreact, to become too emotional, to lose my cool, and to let my anger rise past the boiling point. When I mouth off and bark back at people, the tension doesn't subside to allow reason and understanding to prevail. Too often, I personalize the issue—it's me against my enemy! Then the problem inevitably escalates, and each side parries on defense and thrusts on offense. With this attitude, the outcome has to be a zero-sum game: someone wins and someone loses . . . and I'm determined to come out on top.

I'm learning (slowly, but with some discernible progress) to take a deep breath and ask questions instead of attacking. Questions, of course, can be one form of attack, so I'm trying to avoid questions like, "Why are you so stupid?" or "Didn't you realize you were screwing all this up?" In fact, to avoid questions that can be perceived as threatening, I'm learning to make statements that pursue understanding and open the door to a workable solution, such as, "Tell me what you were thinking," or "Tell me more about what was going on." Then, in a context of dialogue, I can work with the other person(s) toward a solution. No enemies, no accusations, just the pursuit of understanding, support, and a workable solution.

When my anger makes me feel righteous and powerful, I use it to intimidate, to make the other person cower, and to be one-up when the conversation ends. But a change is taking place. As I repeatedly experience grace, my heart is being melted and molded by love. My desperate drive to win at all costs is subsiding, and my fragile ego no longer needs as much bolstering. A stronger sense of security lets me relax and enter into meaningful conversation, and my goal shifts from trying to be one-up to seeking the best for the other person. Sometimes, seeking the best for someone means speaking hard truths about his lies or her irresponsible behavior. But if I'm secure and full of grace, I'll say hard things to help, not to control or punish. There's a huge difference. This is an important and immensely practical lesson for me.

Confront the dark parts of yourself, and work to banish them with illumination and forgiveness. Your willingness to wrestle with your demons will cause your angels to sing. Use the pain as fuel, as a reminder of your strength.

—August Wilson

Years ago, my manager Jay Green occasionally got upset when new directives came down from the corporate office that complicated our lives. Sometimes he got really angry with the faceless, nameless bureaucrats who made those decisions. One time he told me, "Troy, I wrote a letter to the vice president of the company, the one who sent this unreasonable policy to us. I'm putting it in my desk drawer. After forty-eight hours, I'm going to take it out and read it again. If I still feel the same way and think the reasoning makes sense, I'll sign it and send it. But if it doesn't pass the smell test at that point, I'll tear it up and throw it away."

Imagine how it would help if we followed this principle—or something remotely similar. How hard would it be to wait ten minutes to post a response on someone's blog or Facebook page? We might not send half of the edgy messages we send now.

Old habits die hard. I guess I'll always be an emotional person, and I'll always struggle with my tendency to react in anger to any kind of offense. But at least I have learned that I have a choice. I have a picture of my manager putting his emotions and perceptions on hold for a while to see if a cooler head might prevail. And in my mind, I can see the mayor of New York responding to chaos and loss with a wonderful blend of compassion and wisdom. I'm taking some steps to become Rudy Giuliani cool.

LOOK FOR THE GOOD

I've always been a worrier. At home or at work, I couldn't turn my mind off. Fear and doubt fueled more anxiety. It's a good thing to be focused and to think, but it's destructive to see only clouds and no silver linings.

As my business grew, I made enough money to invest in ventures far from my expertise in insurance and business consulting. The economy always has cycles, but in 2008, the cycle headed south at an unprecedented rate. Do you remember the language the broadcasters used to describe it? They said it was "the worst economic catastrophe since the Great Depression." It wasn't a good time to be leveraged in real estate in California. In the blink of an eye, the seemingly always-upward market in our state went into a nosedive, and my property values went with it.

The lesson I learned (and thankfully, I learned fairly quickly) was to get out as quickly and smoothly as possible. I had a wonderful CPA who helped me make wise decisions. I sold property at a loss, but I no longer had to worry about it. I didn't have to wait for an awkward phone call or a knock on the door from someone at the bank.

I've missed more than 9000 shots in my career. I've lost almost 300 games. Twenty-six times I've been trusted to take the game winning shot and missed. I've failed over and over and over again in my life. And that is why I succeed.

—Michael Jordan

Sometimes we have to take two steps back before we can move forward again. On a mountainside, climbers may realize they've come to a dead end. They have to retrace their course back to a place on the cliff where they can find a better route. It will do them no good to stay at the dead end and complain incessantly. The moaning and blaming won't take them one step closer to the peak. But a realistic appraisal and a new plan will get them there.

From my painful experiences in real estate, I made a number of very important discoveries. One is that I can trust my CPA with my life and my future. I had trusted him previously, but in the heat of having to make hard decisions, I found his wisdom, patience, and good nature to be marvelous gifts. And I learned a crucial investment principle: I need to stay in my world of expertise.

In parallel with the insight to focus on my strengths, I've learned to ask more questions on the front end of any business deal. I wanted to trust people implicitly, the way I want people to trust me. But that's not a smart way to live. Before trusting people too quickly, I need to ask as many questions and listen to as many answers as needed so that I feel confident about the person sitting across the table.

I thought I knew the meaning of being a co-guarantor of a note, but it had been only an abstract concept. Now I know what it feels like to be left holding the bag. When the investment collapsed, the other guy didn't have the means to pay off his loan. So as far as the bank was concerned, it was like my name was the only one on the document, and they focused on getting their money from me. I thought they'd squeeze him to get what they could before coming to me. They didn't. I had a bull's-eye on my chest. It was like the other guy never existed. Now I know.

Failure has humbled me, at least a little. I've realized I may be considered an expert in one or two fields, but I'm a novice in so many others. Now, I ask questions—to gain information, but also, to test other people to see if they're trustworthy.

*So many ideas come to you (when slumping as a hitter), and you
want to try them all but you can't. You're like a mosquito in a
nudist camp. You don't know where to start.*

—**Reggie Jackson**

NEVER TOO LATE

Some people live under a cloud because they believe they've messed
up so badly or so long that their lives will never get back on track.
Sometimes the most gregarious people are covering up their insecurity
and those who appear fearless are secretly terrified they'll be exposed
as failures. Smiles and bravado may be very real, but they also could be
masks people wear to cover up their deep sense of worthlessness and
helplessness.

No matter what dumb things you've done, and no matter what has
been done to you, there's always hope that you can turn tragedy into real
progress. The only irreparable damage is the harm you're not willing to
examine and learn from.

But let's be honest: Not everyone learns from mistakes and heartaches, and no one learns from them quickly or completely. We're all works
in progress, and our responses are often as flawed as the perceptions or
behavior that contributed to the problem in the first place. Still, we need
confidence that our difficulties, whatever the cause, will somehow produce something good in us. In his book, *Leadership Pain*, my friend Sam
Chand offers a strong hope and a warning:

Failure isn't the end of the world for those who are open to God's
tender, strong hand. It's the beginning of a new wave of insight,

creativity, and effectiveness—but only if we pay attention and learn the lessons God has for us. When we receive a vision from God, we're excited, and we dream about the steps it will take to fulfill it. We generally assume God will supply everything to accomplish the goal he's given to us, but we often fail to realize that he needs to do a deeper work in us so we can do what he has called us to do. And the way he works deeply in us is through all kinds of opposition, stress, heartache, loss, and obstacles. In other words, God works most powerfully in and through our failures.[30]

Pain is often a severe but effective tutor. In the middle of heartache, we have a choice: to become more humble and open, or to be defiant and closed. It's our choice, and the quality of the rest of our lives depends on our response. If we look for the good, we may have to dig a long way before we discover the treasure of wisdom and strength. And in fact, the treasure we find may be very different from anything we expected. We were looking for relief, but we found insight; we were searching for escape, but we found a new source of security.

Many of us have skipped this school for a long time. We avoided the curriculum of suffering and heartache, and our truancy only compounded the problem. It's never too late to go back to class, to learn the lessons we need to learn to live a richer, more fulfilling life based on rigorous honesty, real wisdom, and genuine relationships. Life has a way of returning us to the lessons we've yet to learn.

I've certainly had ups and downs in business. Through the years our agency has been very consistent, but my consulting clients come and go for a number of reasons. Sometimes the needs of companies change, and sometimes leadership changes. At every point, I've learned some valuable lessons and reinvented myself so I could be more effective with my next clients. Thankfully, I've always had plenty of business.

Early in my consulting career, I got upset when things didn't work out with a company I was helping, but I soon discovered that the normal process of business includes predictable and unpredictable cycles. The railroad tracks to success are never perfectly straight. Over time I became more comfortable with the curves and hills, so I didn't jump off when I hit a bump or two.

It's not how far you fall, but how high you bounce that counts.

—Zig Ziglar

LIMITS

In our most important relationships, we can make opposite errors: caring too little or caring too much. When someone we love is hurting, it's good and right to provide comfort. When he's wandering, we can step in to offer words of wisdom. When she needs a hand to get through a rough patch, we can offer assistance. But there are times when helping is hurting, when our care for others prevents them from gaining wisdom from the consequences of their behavior. When we take responsibility for their feelings and behavior—bailing them out, making excuses for them, and believing their lies—we do much more harm than good.

After speaking at an event in Canada, I was on a flight home and sitting next to a nicely dressed lady who, I could tell from the papers she was reading, was an executive in the high-tech world. Before we took off, the attendant asked if we had any drink orders. She ordered a drink; I asked for water. A few minutes later, the attendant brought our drinks. I smiled at the lady next to me and said, "That's my favorite drink."

She smiled back and said, "Well, you should have ordered one too. You'd enjoy it."

I used one of my favorite lines. I told her, "My sponsor, my family, and my friends wouldn't appreciate it if I joined you." She laughed, which was my intended response, and I continued. "Actually, I don't even have the urge anymore."

She asked the obvious question: "Are you an alcoholic?"

I said, "Yes, I'm the worst kind: I prefer to drink alone."

This brief but honest conversation opened the door for her to share more of her life. She told me, "Before I got on this flight, my son called and asked me to pay for him to go to a very expensive rehab clinic in Malibu." I nodded. I've heard this story many, many times. She then said, "I'm more than willing to help. His dad was an alcoholic and died when he was very young." She paused for a second, and then added, "But he said something that really bothered me. He said he wanted to go to the clinic for twenty-eight days, and when he got out, he promised he'd drink responsibly."

I've heard that part of the story many times, too. To her credit, she didn't buy his reasoning. She explained, "I told him I'm not willing to pay tens of thousands of dollars for him to have a vacation at one of the most expensive clinics in the country, and then go back to drinking again."

A person's addiction to alcohol, drugs, gambling, sex, porn, shopping, or whatever, affects everyone in the family. In different ways, they all can be living a lie by avoiding responsibility for their flaws or taking too much responsibility for another's flaws. It's a crazy-maker. Someone who finds enough courage and wisdom needs to speak the truth, set limits, and offer a way forward. Sometimes it's the addict, but often it's someone else in the family who stops the spiral of destruction. One person can take bold steps toward emotional and relational health. This person can offer a path forward for the whole family, but there are no guarantees anyone else will follow.

When adversity strikes, that's when you have to be the most
calm. Take a step back, stay strong, stay grounded and press on.

—*LL Cool J*

FILLING DEEP HOLES

I was only five when my father died in a car wreck. I have very few
memories of him, but from all accounts, he was both wonderful and deeply flawed. Dad was an alcoholic, which was the cause of his car wreck, but
he was also witty and a good provider. He grew up on a farm in north-
ern Minnesota. In case you can't tell from my name, my dad's family is
Norwegian. When he came of age, he joined the Marines and was based
at Camp Pendleton near Oceanside in southern California. He fought on
the front lines in the Korean War, where the Marines were in some of the
toughest battles in the conflict. He was a man's man, and I would have
loved to live under his arm all my life. But that didn't happen.

Undoubtedly, the loss for my mother and the five kids was sudden
and devastating. Our hero and provider was ripped from us in an instant.
He had lived through brutal combat, but he died on an American high-
way. My mother could have collapsed in grief, and she could have felt the
burden of raising five little kids was too much to bear, but she found a way
to create a stable, happy, loving home for us. Even though all my friends
had dads, I never felt shortchanged in the least.

My mother became our hero and provider. She didn't feel sorry for
herself. She didn't try to escape, and she didn't put unrealistic demands
on us. Our home was marked by creativity and spontaneity; in it, the kids
thrived. Over the years, all five of us have endured the full range of difficulties and failures, but in each instance, the rest have rallied to provide
support and care.

We all experienced a deep hole when Dad died, but Mom filled it with affection, laughter, and stimulating conversation. Life in our home was never dull. We owe her so much. The loss of one person can create a deep gash in the soul of an individual and a family, but the love of one person can fill and heal a gaping wound. I want to be that kind of loving person for the rest of my life.

———————————— ❖ ————————————

Given the amount of unjust suffering and unhappiness in the world, I am deeply grateful for, sometimes even perplexed by, how much misery I have been spared.

—**Dennis Prager**

AT THE BRINK

When my children, Michael and Emily, were five and four years old respectively, they contracted Guillain-Barre syndrome. It's a virus that attacks the nervous system, leaving the victim paralyzed and unable to talk. No antibiotic works on a virus; it has to run its course. Michael got it first. He was in the hospital for three months and then in therapy for ten months to relearn how to walk and talk. About a year later, Emily contracted the disease. Initially, she was in the hospital for three months, and then she required therapy for eleven months. Two months after she was released, she had a relapse. This time, the disease was even worse. Everyone was shocked when it reappeared. The doctors from Stanford and the University of Southern California both said the odds of a child getting it again were astronomical . . . but it happened to my Emily.

For my wife and me, daily trips to the hospital lasted almost three years. The drive was forty-five minutes each way. The physical toll, though, was nothing compared to the emotional weight of each day. It's one thing to watch an elderly person suffer and deteriorate, but it's even more excruciating to watch your little children struggle to communicate because a dread disease has robbed them of their childhood and their happiness.

I often felt like I was on the brink of exhaustion and collapse. At one point, my mother came to be with us in the hospital. Out in the hall, she told me, "Son, you look so tired. I don't know how you're getting through this."

I responded, "Yeah, I don't see any end in sight. This is either going to make me or break me."

Never confuse a single defeat with a final defeat.

—F. Scott Fitzgerald

In our most painful and difficult situations, we don't want to learn any lessons. We just want our kids to be well, and we want to survive another day. The day we took Michael to the emergency room after he first showed symptoms, I'd never heard of Guillain-Barre syndrome. The ER doctor called for a neurologist to examine my five-year old. Dr. Isabelo Artacho soon came to the room and looked carefully at Michael. His first words to me were, "Mr. Korsgaden, we need to perform more tests to determine what's wrong with your son."

Before he could say anything else, I verbally grabbed him by the lapels and barked, "I'll pay anything! Just get him the help he needs!"

He looked me in the eyes and said calmly, "Money isn't the issue. Mr. Korsgaden, you need to calm down. Your money has no bearing on our treatment."

I was slow to grasp what he meant. I insisted, "Yeah, but I'll pay whatever it takes to get him the care he needs. Bring in *any* specialists!"

Again, he explained clearly and politely, "Sir, money won't solve the situation. We're doing everything we can. Please calm down."

The doctors soon identified the cause of Michael's problem, and they instituted a treatment plan. Not long after he entered the hospital, I made the kind of vow soldiers under fire make in foxholes. I made a deal with God and anyone else who was interested. I swore I'd work fewer hours and spend more time with my family. I was as sincere as I could be, but by the time Emily came down with symptoms almost a year later, I was working just as many hours. My vow hadn't stuck.

As I look back on my life, I realize I've made vows during times of distress, and I've broken most of them when the pressure was relieved. That's human nature, but my trajectory of learning has been upward. Gradually, maybe imperceptibly, my vows have become less rash and my commitments more solid.

CLING TO HOPE

No one lives a Disneyland life. We may want it, we may try to engineer it, but life has a way of throwing curveballs at us when we least expect it. If we expect the graph of our lives to move only up and to the right, we'll be disappointed, maybe shattered, when we encounter setbacks. We'll want to scream, "This isn't fair!"

A far more realistic and mature approach is to have what one leader called "ambidextrous faith," accepting pleasures and blessings with our right hands and difficulties in our left, and trusting that God will use both to accomplish His purposes in our lives.[31]

Success is most often achieved by those who don't know that
failure is inevitable.

—Coco Chanel

At a funeral for a young man in our community, a grieving and distressed person asked the pastor, "Why would God let something like this happen?"

The pastor obviously had heard similar questions many times over the years, and he had an answer that may or may not have satisfied the angry, anxious person. He said, "Some things in this life are difficult, and we have no answer to explain the cause or God's reason for allowing them. They're a mystery to us." He paused for a second, and then he said something very profound: "But we also don't have a reason for all the *good things* God pours into our lives. We don't deserve them. They're a mystery to us, too."

Sometimes, we have to work really hard to cling to hope. After Emily spent three months in the hospital and another eight in therapy with Guillain-Barre, we thought we were finally out of the woods. We had both children at home, and we could try to create a sense of normalcy. Then, three months later, a few weeks before Christmas, Emily's head began to rock back. The disease had returned, and she went back into the hospital. We were crushed.

The worry and fear of having a very sick child, coupled with the excruciating grind of spending hours in the hospital every day, took a heavy toll on all of us. But then, another complication arose. During Emily's stay, a measles outbreak caused the hospital to institute a policy that no children could come into the hospital unless they were sick. In other words, Michael couldn't visit Emily while she was in the hospital. All three times the disease was diagnosed, once for Michael and now twice for Emily, the doctors told us sadly, "You need to be prepared. Recovery could take up to a year."

My wife and I took turns at home with Michael and at the hospital with Emily. Christmas was approaching, and my wife announced with a blend of confidence and defiance, "We've missed Christmas for the last two years. We're going to have Christmas this year!"

I brought home a big tree for downstairs and a smaller one for the upstairs. On Christmas Eve, we came home from the hospital and wrapped all the presents. We wanted Michael to have a nice Christmas.

The next morning I heard little footsteps on the stairs. I went out and found Michael. He was crying. I explained, "Michael, don't cry. Santa came to see you. You'll see."

I was completely mistaken about the source of his tears. He looked at me with his big, teary eyes and said, "Dad, I'm really sad."

As I hugged him, he told me, "I'm not crying about Santa. I'm sad because Emily can't be with us on Christmas."

In our family's darkest moment, a child's love shone as the brightest light.

When we assume we can guarantee success, blessings, love, health, and beauty, we will inevitably be shattered by the difficulties we encounter. But if we hold these things loosely, thankful for the good and looking beneath the surface to find light even in dark times, we'll develop a powerful combination of humility, wisdom, and tenacity.

We're flawed people in a flawed world. There are no guarantees of success, comfort, and applause, but if we dig deep, we can live with the certainty that life matters. Whatever your religious persuasion may be, or if you don't have one at all, we all go through seasons in our lives. Perspective makes all the difference. Even when success is elusive, we can still be sane . . . and more than sane, we can become wise and strong.

Failure should be our teacher, not our undertaker. Failure is delay, not defeat. It is a temporary detour, not a dead end. Failure is something we can avoid only by saying nothing, doing nothing, and being nothing.

—Denis Waitley

THINK ABOUT IT . . .

1. Do you typically overreact or underreact in a crisis? Give some examples.

2. How would you describe "Rudy Giuliani cool"?

3. How would calmly asking questions instead of barking accusations or fading into the wallpaper help in tense conversations?

4. Why is it essential to look underneath the confusion and pain to find the treasures of wisdom and strength in difficult seasons of life?

5. What is "ambidextrous faith"? How would it help you respond in the good times and the bad?

| # GREAT TEAM, GREAT LIFE

None of us is as smart as all of us.

—Ken Blanchard

You can lose your mind by trying to make everything work all by yourself. If you're a very small operation, a limited personnel strategy might work for a while, but as your business grows, the work inevitably will become too much for you. You'll burn out or drop dead. Neither of those are good outcomes, no matter how you look at them. But you can also lose your mind by hiring people . . . the wrong people. Over the years, I've hired some of the most wonderful people I've had the privilege to know, but I've also hired a few who drove me nuts. Success and sanity result from finding, enlisting, training, and supervising a great team.

Sometimes people have been in roles for years, but they simply don't fit their positions. As I travel around the country, one of the most common conversations I have begins with an insurance executive saying, "Troy, I've got this employee. She's been with me for fifteen years, and she's a great person. (This statement signals a real problem is about to be revealed.) She doesn't have a license, and when I've told her she needs one, she says, 'I haven't had a license in all these years and things have worked out just fine. I don't need one.' What should I tell her?"

"It's easy," I answer. "Tell her she needs to get a license because it's the law."

"But, but, what if she still is resistant?"

"Then tell her that she needs to find work where her desires and goals fit the business. We're professionals, and professionals in our industry are required to have licenses."

The boss often winces and then tells me, "Yeah, but she knows so many people in our community, and people often tell me how helpful she is when they come to our office. I'm afraid of the collateral damage if I have to let her go."

I immediately assure him, "It will be minimal, if any."

The leader usually looks stunned at my reply, so I explain. "People buy your products and services for any of a number of reasons. Customer service is certainly one factor, but it's only one of them. Most people don't make their buying decisions because of the person who greets them at the door or sits at a desk. What you offer the public has intrinsic value, and your company has a good reputation. Those are your most important selling points to the public. Your employee isn't indispensable. Who knows, you might hire someone who is better at customer service than the woman who refuses to be professional."

This conversation is similar for all leaders in virtually all companies. We've been nice and compliant to the wishes of a staff member or two for a long, long time, but at some point, our professional integrity pushes us to be clear about the requirements for the job. If the staff member doesn't want to be a professional, you have your answer. No arguing, no blaming, and no confusion. You are required—by your stockholders, your CEO, your partners, your bylaws, or your team—to lead with integrity and courage. Dr. Sam Chand is one of the world's most gifted leadership consultants. He remarked that he has never consulted with the head of any organization that didn't need to fire someone.

"Right firing" is just as important as "right hiring."

Everybody can be replaced. All of us are expendable. When I speak on this topic, I often tell the audience that if I catch a plane to St. Louis after my talk that day, and it crashes, a few people will miss me, but the thousands of customers of Korsgaden/Jansma Insurance Agency will remain loyal to the company. Sharon and the rest of our fine staff members will keep things going and provide superior service just like they always have. I sure hope a few people will wish I was still around, but our customer service won't miss a beat.

To me, teamwork is the beauty of our sport, where you have five acting as one. You become selfless.

—**Mike Krzyzewski**

RECRUITING

People leave a staff team for any number of reasons: to get married, move to other communities, have babies, retire, or go back to school. A few get terminal illnesses. Some of them grow old and die. Sometimes a relative becomes an addict and the employee wants to devote her life to his recovery, or a staff member wants to start a business. When one person leaves, we need to be ready to find the "next man up," as they say in professional football when a key player is hurt.

We need to pay attention to the world of business because it's changing rapidly. In the personal services industries, we either need to align with other companies that provide specialization of services to meet every need in customers' lives, or we have to hire and train people in our offices to be specialists—this is part of "the omni channel." *Omni* means "all" in Latin. The omni channel includes people, technology, and systems: providing services in person, online, by phone, instant messaging, and through other avenues. The options are expanding rapidly. Stay tuned; the next breakthrough technology to contact customers is always right around the corner. We provide a wide range of possibilities, and customers decide how they want to access the services. Outsourcing or insourcing . . . either way works, but you have to provide one or the other or you'll be left in the dust.

Today, people increasingly expect exemplary, tailored, specialized service. Let me give an example. I won an award, which included an all-expense paid trip to Puerto Rico for my wife Janette and me. To prepare for the trip, she went online to the Macy's site to look at dresses, shorts, tops, shoes, and more things than I can list. Of course, all of the clothes needed to be the latest style. A few days later, the truck pulled up in front of our house. I think the delivery guy could have used a front-end loader, but he made several trips to carry all the boxes to the door.

Janette spent hours opening boxes and trying on the new clothes. She loved some, liked some, and didn't like a lot of them. A day or two later, she announced, "Does anyone want to drive down to Macy's with me? I need to return a few things." Everyone wanted to go, so we piled the boxes in the back of the car and piled ourselves in the seats for the trip to the mall.

When we arrived, it took all of us to carry the boxes into the store. When we put them down on the counter, the saleslady didn't miss a beat. I think she'd seen this movie before. My wife told her, "I bought a lot of things online, but these are the ones that don't fit or I don't want. I'd like to return them."

No problem. The lady smiled, took out her laser gun, and began shooting all the bar codes on the stacks of boxes to reverse the charges to my credit card. As she finished, she looked at Janette and asked, "You may want to look at some other items in our store that might work for you. We have a personal shopper who will be glad to help you. The service is free. She assists people in finding just the right styles and colors of clothes. Would you like her help?"

Janette prefers to do her own shopping, so she replied, "Thanks, but I don't think so. I'd rather shop alone." Janette tried on and bought some beautiful clothes. In fact, we walked out with twice as many boxes as we had come in with. I thought we might have to call the delivery guy to see if he could find that front-end loader. Janette was thrilled. As we drove away, I wondered if she would have bought more or less if she'd used the store's personal shopper. I don't think she would have (or could have) bought any more!

On the other hand, my sisters Sharon and Stacy love to use Macy's personal shopper. Before they go to the store, they call to make an appointment. When they arrive, the personal shopper takes them into a private room and asks great questions. When she finds out what they want, she brings in all kinds of gorgeous clothes for them to try on. They thoroughly enjoy the attention and the expertise. For them, it's a clothes spa!

Macy's is an omni channel, providing a full range of specialized services: online, in the store on the racks, and in the store with a personal shopper. Janette is a loyal customer who prefers to shop online or in person, but Stacy and Sharon enjoy using the services of a personal shopper.

Organizations exist only for one purpose: to help people reach ends together that they couldn't achieve individually.

—Robert H. Waterman

Let me explain how the principle of specialization works in our office. We're in the insurance business, and we offer many different types of insurance. In the past, we were all generalists, but we've trained each of our staff to be an expert in one specific area. A *generalist* would need to know everything about everything, but that's not practical in an increasingly complex world of insurance. A *specialist* needs to have in-depth knowledge of the details of one type of insurance, the savvy to know how to find answers to complex problems, and a working knowledge of company policies. In addition, the specialist is the go-to staff member for that line of insurance and has the responsibility to meet sales goals for his or her product line.

It works beautifully: When an auto insurance customer asks about life insurance, the auto specialist goes to our life specialist to get the information and returns to share it. Or, if the situation is complicated, she asks the life specialist to meet with her and the customer. We never pass a customer off to someone else. The employee who initially serves the customer stays with him or her throughout the process. Relationships are everything. We want our staff members to build quality relationships with the people who come to see them, and they can't develop understanding and trust if we pass people off to other specialists. Each of our people becomes a switchboard, gathering information and resources from other specialists while providing exemplary service. The people on our staff don't have to be experts at *everything*, but they must become experts in *one thing*. This has proven to be a very effective way to structure our company.[32]

Our customers, however, have desires and needs that are far beyond what we can provide. If we want to be a comprehensive omni channel, we could hire a real estate agent, an attorney, a CPA, and a doctor to be on our staff, but that's not our mission. Providing great insurance service *is* our mission, so we've created a network of competent, trusted professionals in our community. In annual reviews or in any conversation, we may find that a customer needs a good doctor, or wants to buy or sell a house, has inherited a lot of money and needs a tax attorney, or may be new to the community and wants a recommendation about a grocery store or a dry cleaner. We've screened professionals and stores in our community, and we refer our customers to them. And of course, when they hear their clients, customers, and patients talk about our referral, they refer people to us. It's a sweet arrangement, but it doesn't happen by magic. We have to train our people to think about specialization.

Doctors routinely practice specialization. My physician in Los Angeles, Dr. Tommy Tomazowa, is a world-class doctor. He's not a heart specialist, but he knows one. He's not an oncologist or an orthopedic surgeon or a gastroenterologist or any of the other specialists people often need, but he has identified doctors he trusts, and he refers his patients to them. If he tried to do it all—or if he claimed he could do it all—he'd lose credibility and his patients would leave him in droves. Referring to the right specialists builds trust, and consequently, it builds his practice.

The leaders who work most effectively, it seems to me, never say "I." And that's not because they have trained themselves not to say "I." They don't think "I." They think "we"; they think "team." They understand their job to be to make the team function. They accept responsibility and don't sidestep it, but "we" gets the credit. . . . This is what creates trust, what enables you to get the task done.

—Peter Drucker

NON-NEGOTIABLES IN HIRING

Because it's always possible that one of our people will leave our team for some reason, Sharon and I constantly have our eyes open to recruit the next right person.

Think of every person you meet as a prospective client, a prospective employee, or both. Condition yourself to scout for potential employees wherever you are. It could be the waitress at the coffee shop, the clerk at the bank, or the concierge in your local hotel—someone who provides excellent customer service, who has a great attitude, who does whatever is needed to get the job done and who does it with a smile. That's the kind of person you want working for you.

For instance, when I see someone who gives exemplary service, I often compliment him or her and try to find out what's under the surface. It's not an in-depth interview by any means. Sometimes I lean over the counter and tell an especially positive person, "If you're ever looking for a place where you can make more money and have more fun, come see me. We aren't hiring right now, but we will be in the very near future. I like your attitude, and I think you would fit right in with my team." I give the person my card and walk away. Nothing in the world may come of this brief encounter, but at least I've encouraged someone who's doing a great job. Then again, sometimes the person shows up in our office the next day.

Your goal in these first conversations is only to make initial contact. To avoid the appearance of stealing prize employees from fellow business-people in your area, don't mention work to them a second time. If they contact you, however, you can consider them fair game.

Some business leaders assume they can put an ad in the paper or post a position online, and the right person will magically appear. Sure, it happens, but it's the exception, not the rule. Years ago I read Don Martin's *Team Think*, a book that compares recruiting new employees to scouting the best players in sports.[33] I asked a friend of mine to name his favorite sports team. He said it was his college football team. I asked, "Is it possible the team may need a top-rated quarterback in the next few years?"

Without hesitation he said, "Yeah, their quarterback just graduated, and they really need to find a great one if they want to compete in the conference—to say nothing of trying to win a national title."

I asked, "Did your head coach put an ad in the paper?"

He laughed. "Of course not. They have three already on the team, and they've already signed the best prospect in the country. The problem is that he's a junior in high school, so he won't be eligible for another year."

I smiled and said, "That's exactly my point. Your coach and his staff aren't sitting around waiting for someone to appear and fill a key spot on the team. They're always searching, looking for the best players, and they're looking for them before they can even attend college. That's the way to find the best college football stars, and it's the best way to find team members for our companies."

It's easy to get good players. Getting them to play together, that's the hard part.

—Casey Stengel

When Sharon and I talk with prospective team members, we look for two traits we've learned to value over the years: a positive attitude and a genuine desire to grow. Plenty of people are nice, but they don't have much drive. And a lot of people have drive, but they're, well, not very pleasant to be around. Both qualities are essential . . . absolutely essential, with no hedging, no compromises, no excuses, and no effort on our part to try to make a square peg fit into a round hole.

We've had very pleasant people who had no vision for personal development, and we've had brilliant, driven employees who had caustic spirits. We've learned that we can't settle for one without the other. We can train people to do all kinds of things, but we can't train them to be pleasant, and we can't train them to want to grow. Those are intrinsic character traits . . . or not.

In the interview process, don't rush to fill the slot. I've seldom talked to any business leader who regretted being thorough in hiring key staff members. Ask questions that reveal the two non-negotiables, and look for authenticity in attitude and drive.

Let's be honest. Some people in our offices have very finely tuned antennas to pick up unspoken but very real messages, but others among us are dense. A corporate leader explained, "I'm always part of the interview process, but I've discovered something about myself: I'm much too positive—you could say naïve—about people. If they smile and say they want to work for us, I'm ready to make an offer! But I have two staff members who have an uncanny ability to perceive a person's real character. After I meet with a prospective hire, I send him to those two. When I get a thumbs-up, a thumbs-down, or a set of questions from my two staff members to explore further with the person being considered, I pay attention. I need those two so I don't make dumb decisions in hiring!"

I am a lot like the dense corporate leader. If a person comes into my office for an interview and says, "I like your office," I assume she's very perceptive. If she remarks, "I like your computer," I think, *She's up to date with the latest technology.* If she says, "I think I'd like to work here," I reply, "Great! You're hired. Don't even go home. You can start right now!" I can't figure out why she's laughing when she walks out of my office, and later, I wonder why she's stalking me!

ONBOARDING

When people are hired, I assume they're coming as a blank slate. They may know a lot about the business, but they still need to know the particulars about *our* business. And many people have only a rudimentary understanding of the insurance industry. We first give them an orientation about the history of the company to provide context for what we do all day every day. The company didn't drop out of the sky this morning. It has a long and rich history—full of characters, plot twists, and heroes. People need to know how they fit into this story.

The new hires then need a thorough grasp of the operating system in the office: communications, data, flow of information, decision points, the responsibilities of each person on the team, and what to do when they have questions or problems. This, of course, takes more than a few minutes to explain, and it often takes days or even weeks for the new people to get the hang of the system. Learning a new system and feeling comfortable and proficient in a new culture require the two essential traits. They'll encounter confusion and frustration, so they need a positive attitude and the drive to excel.

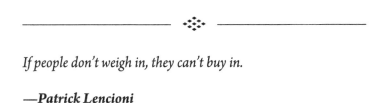

If people don't weigh in, they can't buy in.

—Patrick Lencioni

DEVELOPING THE TEAM

In *Power Position Your Agency*, I describe the elements and the process of creating an outstanding team in our industry. Here, I want to hit the high points and apply them to virtually all fields of business.

The key player

One of the most important principles I discovered was the need to hire someone to make me more effective. I came to a point when I had packed every minute of every day with essential tasks and appointments. I no longer had a minute to spare, and the burden of keeping up with every detail was killing me. I needed help!

The solution was an epiphany. I realized I could hire a person, even a part-time person, to make appointments, confirm the appointments, and fill in any gaps in my schedule by calling other customers to meet with me. This person is our Agency Contact Representative (ACR). We developed scripts she could use, and we dove in. It worked even better than I'd ever dreamed! We work together to identify people I want to see, either she or I make the appointments, and she calls the day before to confirm the time and place.

As this process started and worked so well, I began to operate with freedom and confidence that each day would be more productive than ever. The system can be tailored for any business. This person is the "option quarterback" in the office who is always looking for an opening to make a big play.

I recommend linking the ACR's schedule with your schedule on your phone. She can also provide, on paper or online, the daily schedule with updated entries for upcoming days and weeks. She can have the scheduled people fill out any information forms before they arrive, and possibly have those forms sent to you before the appointment. Afterward, she can enter the forms in the database for customers' files. In addition, the ACR should always be on the lookout for any information that will help you be more personal and informed, such as a recent marriage, a new baby, a recent claim, a new car, a second home, or whatever might be good to know.

The ACR will become your voice and face, so it's crucial to find someone who represents you exceptionally well. In fact, this may be the most important role in your company. Find someone who is the epitome of the two characteristics we've identified, pleasant and professional, and be sure this person fully understands and has bought into your business philosophy, goals, and culture. I've found that some of the best people for this role come from outside the company for two reasons: outsiders are more sensitive to the public perceptions of you and your company, and they aren't embroiled in any insider drama in your office. Higher sensitivity and fewer distractions—not a bad way to stay focused on the job you want her to do.

In every business, leaders who want an ACR need to ask themselves,

- What is the heart of my effectiveness?

- What puts me in front of the most people in the most effective way?

- How can I structure a role that maximizes my time and multiplies my impact?

- Where will I find the right person for this role?

- How will this person fit into our team?

The answers to these questions may be very different for a dentist's office than a plumbing company, and they're different for a real estate agency than a dress shop. But the questions are certainly worth answering.

This person is the lifeblood of growth for your company. You're not doomed if you don't have someone in this role, but you'll almost certainly flourish if you have one.

It is amazing how much you can accomplish when it doesn't matter who gets the credit.

—Robert Yates

Replace yourself

The only way to grow a business is to generate more revenue and net a higher profit. At some point, you're maxed out, so you need to multiply yourself. Computers have increased our productivity, but they have their limits. In all personal services industries, and in most other companies, the answer is to hire more competent people.

The ACR helped me be far more streamlined and effective in meeting with people and providing for their insurance needs. Our business was booming! Hiring the right person to help me worked so well to reduce stress and make me more effective that I took it another step: I decided to replace myself. Even with the ACR maximizing my days, I still had too much to do each day. In my business, personal contact is everything. The only way I could free up more time was to hire someone to manage our day-to-day business.

In fact, I adopted a crucial principle that has transformed our business: If you have a job to do and you can hire someone to do it, make the hire! But at every point, go through the process to hire the right person.

To serve as our Office Director and oversee the operations of every aspect of the enterprise, I needed someone who is brilliant, competent, gracious, diplomatic, and thorough. I could have searched for someone with those traits and skills in the top companies in America, but I didn't have to look that far. My sister Sharon perfectly fit the bill, and she's doing an incredible job. In fact, I've made her an equal partner in the agency. Because of her, our company has continued to grow by leaps and bounds. She loves her work, our staff love and trust her, and our customers are getting the finest service we can possibly offer. I live each day knowing that Sharon has my back. I can't tell you how much that means to me. Oh, I'm still very involved in our operations, but I'm not on every line in the organizational chart any longer. I have a partner in managing the operations, and we have a great team. This really works for me! More than ever, I'm enjoying the delicious combination of success and sanity.

Creating a culture

Countless books have been written about creating a great culture in an office and in a company. Let me offer a few points I believe are crucial.

From the first day when a person is hired until the retirement party, every staff member needs to believe what they do matters. The goal of the company isn't to make money; it's to provide goods and services to improve the lives of individuals and families. If staff members are convinced what they do each day changes lives, they'll be devoted to excellence, they'll work as a team, and they'll have a sense of pride in their work. And if they believe this with all their hearts, customers will notice, and the revenue will come.

Clear, compelling convictions about the value of work don't magically appear, and they can't be borrowed. Leaders need to carefully craft a mission statement that tells the team what's most important. Collaboration with the team increases buy-in and cooperation. Quite often, this statement requires time and effort to acquire staff input and then shape it so that it inspires each person's imagination. When it's ready, post it on a prominent wall for everyone to see—even the customers who come to the office for appointments. They may be amazed to know that you care about them more than their money.

To stimulate creativity and teamwork, expose all team members to at least some of the complexities of the problems and opportunities. Ask for their input, even if they aren't directly responsible for the outcome. And as much as possible, involve the responsible staff members in the process so they have ownership and a stake in the effectiveness of any program, policy, task, or event.

One of the questions often faced by those who directly communicate with the public is perceived value. A customer may say, "I got your quote, but I have one from a competitor that costs less." Train your staff to never be defensive, but give them a script that says something like this: "We aren't always the lowest price, but we promise the best price for the best service." You offer two things that have value: a great product and great service. Those features often outweigh a few dollars of savings in the eyes of your customers.

Supervising staff members invariably involves providing goals and standards with regular evaluations—at least yearly reviews for all of the staff and more often for new staff members. The standards aren't just about the nuts and bolts of daily tasks. Your people need to remember that they were hired because you value a positive, can-do attitude and the drive for personal development. Punctuality, appropriate dress, courtesy, and integrity are part of the clearly stated standards, and they become part of the review process.

No matter what kind of culture you create for the members of your team, they aren't going to stay long if you don't pay them fairly. We've made it a policy to pay a competitive salary and a generous bonus for those who put in extra effort. We do this to attract and keep the very best people. Great staff members are worth the additional expense. Their professionalism pays for itself. We also use performance rewards to motivate our staff. These incentives don't have to be huge amounts of money to produce huge amounts of extra effort.

Staff meetings can be the black hole of the week. In some companies and departments, people would rather visit the proctologist than try to act interested in another boring meeting. We try to make our meetings short, interesting, and productive. Some topics are information only, but we ask for input on at least one topic on the list. In our preparations, we allot only a few minutes for each topic, and people on our team know we're going to move at the speed of light. If they want to give input, and we hope they do, they need to give it before we move to the next agenda item. We always end with specific assignments and deadlines. Without these nailed-down details, the meeting has been worthless.[34]

These principles and processes to build a great team contribute tremendously to the success of our company and my own peace of mind. I know we're providing the very best service to the people in our community, and we're creating a culture where our team members can thrive. All of this takes some vision, thought, and planning, but it's well worth it. Sharon and Shelly Williams (our Office Manager) often say, "We don't want any drama. If people on our staff team want drama, there's the door to the theater." And they point to the front door.

To build depth of insight and passion of heart in your team, I recommend using this book as a training tool—not just this chapter, but the whole book. Your people need to understand the pressures they face, the looming specter of burnout, the need for a clear purpose, and the power of strong relationships. They need to see clearly how to plan effectively and put feet to their plans. And they need to realize that the darkest days of their lives just might teach them the most valuable lessons they'll ever learn. Finally, they can see how the mission, values, and roles of the team fit into the overall strategy for your collaborative efforts to provide services and products that will change the lives of the people you serve. That's my hope for you and your team . . . nothing less than that.

———————————— ❖ ————————————

People are like dirt. They can either nourish you and help you grow as a person or they can stunt your growth and make you wilt and die.

—Plato

THINK ABOUT IT . . .

1. How have you seen companies upgrade to provide more specialized services—an omni channel—to customers and clients?

2. What are some ways your company can provide specialization internally? How can you evaluate, select, and offer specialized resources outside your office? How does making referrals to competent professionals help your business?

3. How would hiring someone like my Agency Contact Representative multiply an executive's effectiveness and create opportunities for the whole team?

4. When is hiring more people the right answer to growing a business? What are the appropriate cautions?

5. Look back at the principles under "Creating a culture." Which ones are strengths in your office? Which ones need some attention?

CHAPTER 11 | CELEBRATE EVERY WIN

We can only be said to be alive in those moments when our hearts are conscious of our treasures.

—**Thornton Wilder**

Everything I am, everything I have, and everything I've had the opportunity to do is a gift to me. I'm very grateful for all of that, but I'm even more grateful for the wonderful people who have walked with me as I've encountered the ups and downs of life. Those people have given my life amazing color, volume, and depth. I don't know where I'd be without them. I've mentioned them in other chapters in this book. They are my family, my choir teacher, my first manager, great friends, business leaders I've met along the way, heads of billion dollar companies, and regular people who have stepped into my life when I needed a smile and a kind word.

No one could have had a more ordinary beginning than I did, but no one has been given more opportunities to know and love terrific people and to make a difference in other people's lives. I'm just a kid from a farming town in central California, but I was invited to dine at the Vatican with violins playing as we ate. My kids, Michael, Emily, and Lauren are the finest young people I know. (Yes, I'm a bit prejudiced!) It's a great joy to be with them and see how they're approaching life with joy and courage. I don't deserve this. It's all a wonderful gift. One day when I was thinking about all the blessings I've been given, I told a good friend, "I'm a member of a garage band, but I've been tapped to open for the Rolling Stones!"

When I met Jay Green at his Farmers Insurance office, it didn't matter to me if the company where he worked was the biggest in the world or a rinky-dink outfit. Farmers turned out to be one of the top five insurance companies in America, and number one in about fourteen states. Out of 14,000 agents, our agency has been recognized twice as the top in the country. I'm not the smartest guy among those 14,000, and my office is in a relatively small town amid orange groves, grapes that are dried into raisins, and farmers and ranchers of all descriptions. In our town, you might see a Rolls Royce stopped next to a trailer stacked with hay. I go to church with some wise, witty, and wonderful people. We may not be the most prosperous community in the world, but we have some of the finest people on the planet. How did I get here? My dad moved our family here just months before he died. Coincidence? No, I don't think so. Good luck? It's more than that. It's part of God's mysterious blessing in my life.

I've been given more than enough, and it's my great pleasure to give to others who need assistance. I get perhaps my greatest joy from realizing my gradually transforming perspective on life is having a positive impact on Michael and Emily. I see them draw from a deep well of gratitude, even when things don't always work out the way they hoped. Far earlier than I did, they're learning the joy of generosity. I love to hear them talk about the causes and people they're devoted to help. And I've discovered that children can learn this lesson even earlier. My younger daughter Lauren is, at this writing, seven years old, but she delights to give her attention and love to others. It's a beautiful thing for a father to see.

From no effort on my own, I found myself at the right place and the right time with the right people. I'm so grateful to be where I am.

——————————— ❖ ———————————

Gratitude is when memory is stored in the heart and not in the mind.

—Lionel Hampton

POISON IN THE SOUL

The perception that we deserve more has been with us from the beginning. All people in all cultures at all times have experienced the poison of entitlement. I'm not referring to government programs (though it would be appropriate to address their impact). Instead, we see this perspective saturating our society where people, rich or poor, young or old, believe they have a right to have everything their hearts desire.

The invasive message of advertising, numerous television shows, and far too many of our conversations either boldly or subtly promise we can have it all . . . or rather, we *should* have it all. This expectation—this demand—makes us chronically dissatisfied, wanting more and seldom satisfied. In a magazine interview with Luci Shaw, University of Southern California philosophy professor Dallas Willard remarked,

> We are designed to be creators, initiators, not just receivers. Yet the whole model, the consumerist model of the human being, is to make us passive, and to make us complainers and whiners, because we're not being given what we need. We cook up a "right" to that and then we say we've been deprived of our rights.[35]

We live in the wealthiest country the world has ever known, with conveniences enjoyed by even those at the bottom end of the socioeconomic ladder—a lifestyle that would have been the envy of the rich only a few generations ago. Yet many of us are chronic complainers, comparing our lives with the super-rich and famous, and always (of course) coming up short. Instead of gratitude flooding our hearts and spilling out of our mouths, we moan, grimace, and are jealous that someone else has what we really want.

Actually, having more money and things isn't an effective antidote to the thirst for more. No matter how much we have, we always look up the socioeconomic ladder, not down. If we have a thousand dollars, we're envious of those who have two thousand, and we're dissatisfied until we get there. But if we have a hundred thousand, we're not happy because we know people who have two or three hundred thousand. The process goes on and on. Even most of the wealthiest people on earth don't feel like they have enough. A reporter once asked John D. Rockefeller, the oil tycoon who was the richest man in the world, "How much money is enough?" He replied, "Just a little bit more." Even the baron of industrialism, the person who had amassed the greatest fortune of his day, believed he needed more to be completely happy.

Gratitude is not only the greatest of virtues, but the parent of all the others.

—Cicero

The twin evils of comparison and entitlement rob us of peace, steal our joy, and ruin our relationships because everyone is a competitor. When we see the problem written in black and white, we instantly recognize the grip it has on us, but it retains its stranglehold because these messages are the air we breathe each day.

In light of the enormous push toward unrealistic expectations and demands, gratitude is thoroughly countercultural. It's against the grain. People who want a positive outlook have to be aware of the acidic messages they see and hear each day—and vigorously reject them. Then they need to replace them with messages of hope, love, and thankfulness.

Fortunately, I'm around people with this kind of tenacious gratitude, and I want to be known as one of them, too. We may not be able to change the entire culture, but we can change the atmosphere in our homes and our companies . . . or at least, our small part of our companies. Mahatma Gandhi famously encouraged us, "Be the change you want to see in the world." If our lives are attractive enough, people will ask questions. We don't have to preach with words. Our attitudes and actions do all the preaching that's needed. We can make a difference. It begins with me. It begins with you.

AT THE OFFICE

In our office, Sharon and I have hit on a process of celebrating people. We have a short timeline. We found that if a reward is too far in the future, people lose sight of it, and it no longer is a motivating factor.

In the insurance business, companies give awards for selling your first life policy, selling a dozen in your first year, selling a significant commercial policy, and for almost anything else under the sun. I think they probably give awards for showing up at the office. I have plaques stacked in the closet. But I've noticed that other businesses don't give out awards so freely.

When we saw an article in the paper that a person who works in real estate—an industry that seldom gives awards—was the top salesman for the month, we cut the article out of the paper, took it down to the local trophy shop, and had it mounted under Plexiglas on a piece of wood with an engraved plate that says, "Congratulations from the Korsgaden/ Jansma Insurance Agency!"

At the next weekly meeting of realtors in our city, we asked the emcee if we could make a presentation. We invited the person to come up in front of all the people, and I enthusiastically explained, "We saw the article in the paper that John had done something special, and we want to celebrate with him by giving him this award." I handed him the plaque and announced, "John, great job! Congratulations!" Everybody in the room applauded, and John beamed in the glow of appreciation. In real estate, the companies don't give many awards to put on the agents' walls, so as soon as John got back to his office, he grabbed a hammer and nail and hung it in a place of prominence.

Over the years, we've done similar things for a lot of professionals in different fields. This simple act of appreciation builds wonderful relationships between our office and people in the community. It takes so little from us, but it means so much to them.

The world has enough beautiful mountains and meadows, spectacular skies and serene lakes. It has enough lush forests, flowered fields and sandy beaches. It has plenty of stars and the promise of a new sunrise and sunset every day. What the world needs more of is people to appreciate and enjoy it.

—Michael Josephson

We are even more appreciative of our own employees. We celebrate every time we see them doing a stellar job. For instance, a man called to tell me, "Troy, I want you to know that I called your office last week and talked to your claims concierge. She helped us with a claim. We have a policy with you, but this one wasn't even a Farmers claim. She held our hand through the whole process. You see, the other company didn't want to pay the claim, but our Team Member went to bat for us and made it happen. When their adjuster balked, the Team Member pulled out the contract and read it to him over the phone. It turns out she knew the contract better than he did! I want you to know that we got a competing bid from a company for the same insurance we have with you. Their bid is $1500 a year less than yours, but we're not going to switch because your claims service is worth far more than that to me and to our company."

It's easy to celebrate a call like that! But it's not enough just to casually express appreciation and move to the next item on the agenda for a meeting. People feel valued when others make a big deal of their contributions, their character, and their worth to the team. Sometimes we ask everybody to stop and gather in my office so I can share success stories, look in our employees' eyes, and tell them how much I—and all of us—appreciate their kindness, tenacity, and professionalism. And sometimes we have a full-blown party!

When people on our staff do an exceptionally good job, either on a project or with a customer, we reward them with small gifts of thanks. We sometimes give movie tickets and tell the person to take a few hours off to take a friend or spouse to see a film. I may explain, "If anyone asks how you got off, tell them, 'Troy said I'm doing a great job, and he wanted to reward me.'" Of course, they can go whenever they want to go, but they can still take the afternoon off. We also sometimes give gift cards, gas cards, and other tokens to honor great work.

Years ago, I heard of another way to affirm great work. When someone on our team excelled, I wrote a letter of appreciation, sealed it, and handed it to the person. I said, "When you go home tonight, ask your spouse (or child or roommate) to read this letter out loud." In the letter, I described the specific situation and how my staff member solved the problem and gave excellent service. I also explained how much the person meant to our team and to me. This way, everyone sitting at the family dinner table heard my words of affirmation, respect, and value for the member of our team. It's like I was in the room singing our team member's praises.

We find all kinds of ways to affirm people on our team. It sends a message to everyone else that we notice excellence.

Develop an attitude of gratitude, and give thanks for everything that happens to you, knowing that every step forward is a step toward achieving something bigger and better than your current situation.

—Brian Tracy

We regularly bring lunch to the office from one of our favorite restaurants in town or have potluck for our team. They appreciate the gesture, and we often have wonderful conversations during these relaxed times together. In the past, I've sent the rest of the staff out to lunch, and I stayed to answer the phones. This lets them know that I'm willing to do their jobs, and that I understand what it takes to connect with each person who calls. At Christmas, we give our staff a price limit for gifts, and we play a game: when it's your turn, you can pick an unwrapped gift. It's lots of fun.

Years ago I read a book by an author who recommended making the atmosphere at work like a game. If you use baseball as a metaphor, you can talk about first base being a certain goal, second and third bases are the next levels, and home is the ultimate accomplishment for the month or the year. If you choose football, each yard line shows progress toward the end zone. The people on your team may not have played the sport you choose, but they almost certainly understand the rudiments of the game well enough for the analogy to work. (I'd stay away from cricket. I've never understood it.) Each significant step of progress is another moment to celebrate together.

AT HOME

Our spouse and kids experience celebrations most meaningfully when affirmation is expressed in their love languages. Some feel most valued when we speak words of appreciation, but others feel special when we give them hugs or small gifts to say, "Well done!" In any family, we might find the full array of love languages, so we need to become fluent in them all. Know your family and speak each person's special language to communicate, "I'm so proud of you!"

Some psychologists and family therapists suggest parents should communicate ten to twenty positive messages for each corrective one. A number of parents reverse the ratio. They come home from work exhausted and frustrated. They want their homes to be places of rest and tranquility, but their spouse complains about money and the kids complain about virtually everything. The frazzled person either explodes in anger or implodes in discouragement (or vacillates between the two). We have an audience at work, and we know our messages matter. The audience at home is more tender, so our messages there matter even more.

A number of us need to start by working on our marriages. The ratio applies there, too. Instead of finding fault, picking at little errors and omissions, and being a grump, we need to dust off our radar to notice the good things our spouse is doing. Then we can acknowledge and name them—and we can make a point to overlook the attitudes and behaviors that sometimes drive us nuts. As we become more affirming of our spouse, we can be more affirming of our kids.

If we can gradually change the atmosphere of the home from caustic to affirming, amazing things can happen. Our spouse may not be so critical, and our kids may actually listen when we talk to them. In addition, a more positive outlook changes *us*, probably before it changes the people around us. We become more relaxed, more grateful, and more optimistic. We aren't as threatened by mistakes—ours or others'—so we respond with grace and wisdom instead of blustering or hiding.

The process is clear: Notice the ratio. Change the ratio.

I feel a very unusual sensation—if it's not indigestion, I think it must be gratitude.

—Benjamin Disraeli

In human relationships, and especially in family relationships, there are no guarantees that affirming words will change the world. But it's almost a certainty that the wrong ratio of negative messages to positive ones will crush souls, erode trust, fuel anger, and divide people. Meaningful change always takes hard work and great patience. We need both of those qualities if we're going to change the culture under our roofs.

AT ALL COSTS

Genuine affirmation and celebration have a powerful impact on people, but the same words spoken insincerely have the polar opposite effect. I know. I've done it. Sometimes I can be too positive. I've been so encouraging and appreciative that people at the office and at home have been shocked when I spoke words of correction, even the mildest correction.

I've had team members in my office tell me, "I deserve a raise because you've said I'm doing such a good job."

I respond, "Yes, you are, but that's what I expect of you. I expect all of us to give exemplary service to our customers and work hard to create a great team. You're doing that, and I appreciate it. But you can improve in some areas. Maybe I haven't been as clear about those as I need to be. Let's talk about them."

I think people realize I'm sincere when I tell them how much I appreciate them, but I've also been around leaders and parents whose honey-dripping sentimentality screamed a lack of authenticity. Others have a different problem: the look on their faces and the tone of their voices don't match their words. They say, "Great job," but their non-verbal messages communicate, "I could care less."

When people sense we aren't genuine in our praise, they don't trust *any* of our messages. A chasm opens in the relationship, often leaving us confused because we've "said the right things," while leaving the hearers frustrated and distant.

Genuine affirmation builds an emotional bond. As leaders, however, we need to be careful. Yes, we want to create a very positive environment at work, but our team isn't a real family. We need those people to be profit centers. We value them as human beings with inestimable inherent value, but we've hired them to do a job. Managers sometimes come down on one end of the stick or the other, either treating people on the team like a sibling (or child), or seeing them only as units of production without any value beyond profit and loss. Great managers hold both as important. They treat people with honor and respect, but they also are clear in their expectations of performance. When their people fail, good leaders don't blow a gasket, but they don't overlook it either. They work with people to help them learn from mistakes and become more proficient. But sometimes, for any number of reasons, an employee simply doesn't work out.

We do them no good, and we do the rest of our team great harm, if we put up too long with a bad attitude or poor performance.

Our commitment to family members is deeper, stronger, and more lasting than our relationships to employees. The stakes are higher, the joys are greater, and the pain is more intense. Our love must be sincere, but it isn't simplistic. Love propels us to notice when they do well and tell them how much we appreciate them, but authentic love always seeks what's best for the other person. When they're really messing up, love never ignores or excuses their behavior. We need to separate the person from the performance. We can say, "I love you, but I don't like what you're doing to yourself (or others). In fact, I love you so much that I'm asking you to change."

Silent gratitude isn't much use to anyone.

—Gladys Browyn Stern

Jesus loved everyone, but He said some very hard things to the rebellious and arrogant. He held up a mirror to show them the foolishness in their hearts, and He invited them to experience His love, forgiveness, and acceptance—the surest source of change. Jesus came full of grace and truth. Both—not one or the other. The truth sometimes affirms and sometimes corrects, but people won't accept truth unless it's communicated with grace.

CELEBRATION IS A CHOICE

Many of us have to cultivate the habits of gratitude, affirmation, and celebration. We've been under the gun so long, and we've felt the weight of discouragement for such an extended period that we see dark clouds even on sunny days. At first we have to force ourselves to stop and notice the good things around us, especially in the people closest to us. We may have seen them as threats, but they need to become our treasures.

Take a few minutes at the beginning of each day, either at home or at the office, to jot down the things you're thankful for. Be sure to think of the positive traits of the people you'll see that day. Write them down, too. This exercise only takes a minute or two, but it orients your mind and heart to notice the good and beautiful things you'll see for the rest of the day. Then, begin to point out the traits you appreciate in the people around you. Don't gush, but don't be too hesitant. Simply say, "You did a good job on that," "You handled that situation like a pro," or "Great job on your math test."

Pay attention to the ratio of your messages. If you're giving more than one corrective message for every five affirming ones at the office, begin making adjustments. If you're making more than one in ten or twenty at home, begin overlooking the petty annoyances and point out more of the good things your loved ones are doing. Yes, it'll be hard for some of us at first, but it's amazing how this choice of focus revolutionizes our perspectives. When we become masters of authentic celebration, our hearts will be filled and overflowing, and we'll have an incredibly positive impact on those around us.

You simply will not be the same person two months from now after consciously giving thanks each day for the abundance that exists in your life. And you will have set in motion an ancient spiritual law: the more you have and are grateful for, the more will be given you.

—Sarah Ban Breathnach

THINK ABOUT IT . . .

1. Who are some people you know, in business or in their homes, who genuinely affirm others and celebrate successes? How do the people around them respond in such an environment?

2. How would you describe the impact of comparison and entitlement in the people you know? (No names, please!) How have these twin forces affected you?

3. What are some practical ways you can affirm people and celebrate success at your office?

4. At this moment, what is the ratio of positive to negative messages you communicate in your home? What, if anything, needs to change?

5. What is the impact of insincere appreciation or praise?

6. If celebration is a choice, what steps are you going to take to be more intentional and genuine in affirming and praising the people around you?

CHAPTER 12 | **IT'S YOUR TURN**

Human progress is neither automatic nor inevitable. . . . Every step toward the goal of justice requires sacrifice, suffering, and struggle; the tireless exertions and passionate concern of dedicated individuals.

—Martin Luther King, Jr.

If you want to take your family on a vacation to Yellowstone National Park and the Grand Tetons, you wouldn't immediately pile everyone in the car and leave your house. You'd do some planning . . . maybe a lot of planning. Depending on where you live, it might be more prudent to fly into Salt Lake City, rent a car, and drive a few hours to the West Entrance of Yellowstone. You also need to determine how long you plan to visit those gorgeous sites, where you'll stay, and any excursions you plan to make while you're there.

If you go online, you'll find thousands (maybe millions) of suggestions about hiking trails, campsites, horseback riding, bird watching, fishing, geology tours, rafting, and almost anything else you can imagine. The options are endless, but your time and money aren't.

As the planning proceeds, you'll undoubtedly review your map dozens of times. As you look at it, you'll ask a lot of important questions: How long will it take to get from the airport to the West Entrance? How far is it from there to Old Faithful? How long can we spend on the Grand Loop Road? What time do people see the wolves in the Lamar Valley each evening? Which hikes in the Tetons are best for our family? Where do we need to be each day at lunchtime? What's the typical weather that time of year? And on and on.

A plan, a map, and a schedule give you confidence that the trip will be exactly what you want it to be: thrilling or relaxing, fast-paced or slow. But without the plan, a map, and a schedule, you'll feel tentative, and your family will be confused, anxious, and easily upset.

You're on the verge of an adventure of charting a new future for your life. Actually, you may be in the middle of this adventure, and all you need are some mid-course corrections, but all of us need to look at our life's map to be sure we're going where we want to go.

Of course, a great vacation always has some surprises. A grizzly bear might lumber into the meadow where you've parked, and you decide to stay and watch it for an hour. The delay means you miss a waterfall you planned to see, but you believe seeing a grizzly up close and personal (but not too close) is worth several waterfalls! In our journey to success and sanity, to peace and fulfillment, we need a measure of flexibility as well as good plans. New opportunities arise, crises occur, and a hundred other events surprise us.

The vision must be followed by the venture. It is not enough to stare up the steps—we must step up the stairs.

—**Vance Havner**

FROM A SINGLE SHEET

When I was about twenty-seven, I used a single sheet of paper to write my first roadmap for my career. At the time I'd been in the insurance business about seven years. A good friend, who was also an insurance agent, asked me to come over on a Saturday afternoon to hang out by his pool. It was a gorgeous day. As we ate sandwiches and talked about all kinds of things young men discuss when they sit by a pool, I told him about a book I had just finished reading, *The E-Myth* by Michael Gerber.[36] The author suggested writing a clear, concise plan for your career. As I told my friend about the book, I got excited about the possibility of applying what I'd been reading. I told him, "We need to write a plan for our businesses! If you want to be bigger and better than you are today, you need a plan to take you there. He encourages people to take time to write it down."

My friend paused for a second or two, and then he said, "Let's give it a shot!"

Both of us were really excited about writing our business plan. He ran into his house and came out a few seconds later with two pieces of paper and two pens. He grinned at me and said, "Let's do it, man!"

We each wrote what we wanted our careers to look like down the road. I didn't know if I was planning for the next forty years or the next forty hours. All I knew was that the process of writing clarified my dreams and began to turn them into concrete goals, specific plans, and a schedule I could follow.

My piece of paper had my name in a box in the middle of the page, and I drew lines out to other boxes labeled "home," "fire," "life," "auto," and so on. It was at that moment that I realized I needed to create a great team to work with me.

I began recruiting and hiring some very gifted people, and within eighteen months, my business had doubled in size.

Twenty years later, the friend who was with me that fateful day at his pool came into my office. He sat down across from me and said, "Troy, I've been thinking about those plans we wrote years ago. To be honest, I have very mixed feelings about them."

I was intrigued, and I wondered what in the world he was about to tell me. He continued, "You remember that we both wrote our vision for the future of our businesses." I nodded. "But that's where the similarity ended. That afternoon I put my paper in a desk drawer, and I never looked at it again. You used yours as a template for your future and made it come to life. Today, you and I both see the result of your roadmap in the success of your company. That day by the pool, I had 3000 policies in force, but you had only 1500. Today, I still have 3000, but you have over 8000. I'm very happy for you, but I sure wish I had used my plan like you did."

Whatever course you decide upon, there is always someone to tell you that you are wrong. There are always difficulties arising which tempt you to believe that your critics are right. To map out a course of action and follow it to an end requires courage.

—Ralph Waldo Emerson

He's right about making my plan come to life. That simple exercise by the pool has turned into an annual planning process. Today, our "roadmap to the future" for the agency is about an inch thick and more than 140 pages. Our plans have become far more elaborate for two reasons: we have a far bigger business, and we're far more detailed in our plans. The map has helped tremendously, but I'm still a work in progress—always learning, always growing, always looking for ways to improve.

Don't try to write a 140-page plan on your first try. Start simple. Be sure the one-page version is an expression of your values, your goals, and your passion to succeed. If it is, the results will inspire you to be more expansive and detailed in your next plan, and the process will continue.

We often talk about the need to craft our business plans, but we need clearly articulated plans for our personal lives as well. Again, start simple, and be more elaborate as time goes by, and you see your goals with a sharper eye. What kind of relationships do you want to enjoy with your spouse, children, siblings, parents, and best friends? How can you be more prudent and wise in handling money? What steps do you need to take to care for your body, your mind, and your soul?

Trying to follow my plan has been a mixed bag. In some ways, it's been a roadmap that has taken me places I only dreamed about going in my career. But as I've mentioned frequently in these chapters, I've failed many times and in many ways. I had good intentions to make my family a priority, to exercise and eat right, to cut down on my drinking, and to make other good decisions, but I failed more times than I like to admit. To be perfectly honest, I was more disciplined and determined to follow the roadmap for my business than the one for my personal life. But in the last few years, I've made—and kept—better priorities for my family, my health, and my sanity, and I'm glad for that.

If you don't plan, you'll wander. If you plan, you may still wander a bit, but you'll at least realize it more quickly so you can get back on track.

I have been impressed with the urgency of doing. Knowing is not enough; we must apply. Being willing is not enough, we must do.

—Leonardo da Vinci

THE MOST IMPORTANT FIFTEEN MINUTES

When we invite clients to come to our office for an annual review of their insurance policies and current needs, we promise we won't take more than thirty minutes. Most people are willing to invest this amount of time, but if we asked for more, many wouldn't bother to come. They're afraid they'll be bored to death or we'll ask questions they can't answer. Whatever the reason, we've discovered the promise of a short meeting is as good as gold.

The same principle applies to personal planning. A few crazy people spend hours each week going over and over their business and personal plans. (They may have a diagnosable disorder, but I don't want to throw any stones!) I've found that if people—people in any walk of life, any age, or any status in a company—will invest fifteen minutes in planning at the start of each week, they'll have clearer direction, more confidence, and peace of mind. In that short span of time, you can review what wasn't accomplished the previous week, list the priorities of the coming week, and put those priorities into the schedule. It's amazingly simple and amazingly profitable.

Some items on my list show up every week—not because I don't get them done, but because they're recurring priorities. But many tasks, meetings, and calls are time-sensitive. They have deadlines, and I need to pay attention to them. If I put them on the schedule, they'll probably be accomplished. If they don't show up on my schedule on Monday morning, they're probably toast.

Four steps to achievement: Plan purposefully. Prepare prayerfully. Proceed positively. Pursue persistently.

—William Arthur Ward

NEVER ALONE

Virtually everybody who knows me would describe me as an incredibly self-sufficient guy. Don't believe them. I used to think I could conquer the world on my own, but my false pride and stupidity caused major headaches. We need a full measure of tenacity and grit to keep moving forward, but we also need a running partner or two. I realized I needed a good friend, a mentor, or a coach who could bounce ideas around with me, ask me hard questions, and on more than one occasion, tell me I was about to do something really dumb.

If you don't have someone like this, find one. A consultant or mentor isn't necessarily smarter than you, and it's not someone who has all the answers. More often, it's someone with the wisdom to ask great questions that can help you find the solutions. The people who have helped me most are those who have said, "Troy, let's look at the situation from a different point of view." It's often a perspective that had never dawned on me, but it gave me insight that led to a creative process and a positive conclusion.

At work, in your place of worship, or with close friends, you can form a study group to tackle important issues that you share. The dynamics of interaction often stimulate reflection that goes far beyond an individual's ability to think and plan alone.

We are at our very best, and we are happiest, when we are fully engaged in work we enjoy on the journey toward the goal we've established for ourselves. It gives meaning to our time off and comfort to our sleep. It makes everything else in life so wonderful, so worthwhile.

—Earl Nightingale

TAKE THE STEP

Some people have come to this point in the book and still complain, "Yeah, all these ideas are great, but look at where you are, Troy. I don't have the resources or platform you have." That may be true, but I didn't start where I am today. I was just a kid, a failed musician with no prospects at all. I had the good fortune to meet a wonderful man and asked him for a job. And in the first season of my job, I was a flop! I didn't have a platform . . . and I was blowing up my only hope of one! When I started speaking and consulting, I started from scratch. I had very few contacts, and I had no credibility.

At every stage of my career, I had to make a choice: to stay where I was or to take a risk of stepping out into the unknown. If my career were a baseball game, I'd have to admit that I've struck out plenty of times. But I kept coming up to bat. My friend Duane always says, "We're all in the same ballgame. It's just that some of us are in a different inning." I'd add: "Let's just make sure that we don't take a seventh inning stretch whenever we want to. Sometimes a brief pause turns into a very, very long period of time. It's perfectly fine to pause and rejuvenate, but it doesn't make sense to take a seventh inning stretch and not finish the game."

No matter which inning you're in, and no matter how many times you've hit foul balls, struck out, or made errors in the field, stay in the game and keep playing.

In case you haven't gotten the message so far in the book, let me assure you that I'm not writing as the definitive expert in finding balance, peace, and purpose. I'm in the middle of the process, and I still have a lot to learn. But the lessons I've learned so far have changed my life! As I'm applying the principles in this book, I'm finding more peace of mind than I ever imagined possible. As I experience supernatural love and the security it brings, I can relax. I'm not as anxious. I'm still ambitious, but I'm not as driven. And I'm finding that the joy of giving, in all its forms and to all kinds of people, is what brings the deepest fulfillment and the highest sense of purpose.

Success and sanity are possible. If I can experience them, anyone can.

I think there is something, more important than believing: Action! The world is full of dreamers, there aren't enough who will move ahead and begin to take concrete steps to actualize their vision.

—W. Clement Stone

THINK ABOUT IT . . .

1. Take two pieces of paper and carve out thirty minutes. On one page, write your career goals and create a roadmap to get there. On the other page, write your personal and family goals, and chart out a map to accomplish those goals.

2. On Monday mornings before you do anything else, spend fifteen minutes listing your priorities for the week. Put those in your schedule. Each subsequent Monday morning, update your list and your schedule. How do you think this regular exercise might help you?

3. What are the three most important things you've learned from this book?

4. What is one step you need to take to apply each of them?

ENDNOTES

1 Bob Dylan, "Is Your Love in Vain?" from *Street Legal*, © 1978, Special Rider Music.

2 The Diffusion of Innovation model of Behavioral Change Theory was developed by E. M. Rogers. For more on this model, go to: http://sphweb.bumc.bu.edu/otlt/MPH-Modules/SB/SB721-Models/SB721-Models4.html

3 John Ortberg, *God Is Closer than You Think* (Grand Rapids: Zondervan, 2005), p. 74.

4 "Time to Move On," Tom Petty, from *Wildflowers*, Warner Brothers, 1994.

5 For more about stress and burnout, see Dr. Richard Swenson, *Margin: Restoring Emotional, Physical, Financial and Time Reserves to Our Overloaded Lives* (Colorado Springs: Navpress, 2004).

6 Cited in Stephen E. Ambrose, *Band of Brothers* (New York: Simon & Schuster, 2001), p. 203.

7 "The Perilous Fight," www.pbs.org/perilousfight/psychology/the_mental_toll/

8 Maryann Abendroth, Ph.D., R.N., "Overview and Summary: Compassion Fatigue: Caregivers at Risk," *The Online Journal of Issues in Nursing*, January 2011.

9 For an exhaustive study of the life of Walt Disney, see Neal Gabler's biography, *Walt Disney: The Triumph of the American Imagination* (New York: Vintage, 2006).

10   Cited at jan.ucc.nau.edu/~jsa3/hum355/readings/ellul.htm

11   "Your brain on gambling," Jonah Lehrer, *The Boston Globe*, August 19, 2007.

12   "Running on Empty," Jackson Browne, from *Running on Empty*, © 1977 Asylum.

13   J.I. Packer, *Knowing God* (Downers Grove, IL: Intervarsity Press, 1973), pp. 41-42.

14   Seth Godin, *Linchpin: Are You Indispensable?* (New York: Penguin, 2010).

15   Sarah Young, *Jesus Calling* (Nashville: Thomas Nelson, 2004).

16   "Subterranean Homesick Blues," Bob Dylan, from *Bringing It All Back Home*, © 1965, 1993, Special Rider Music.

17   The Winston ad hasn't been used since 1972, and the Charmin ad was last aired in 1985.

18   For more about Anthony Galie, go to his web site: anthonygalie.com

19   See Neumann, Craig S.; Hare, Robert D., "Psychopathic traits in a large community sample: Links to violence, alcohol use, and intelligence," *Journal of Consulting and Clinical Psychology*, 2008, 76 (5): 893–9.

20   Jim Collins, *Good to Great* (HarperCollins: New York, 2001), p. 41.

21   Gary Chapman, *The Five Love Languages* (Grand Rapids: Zondervan, 2010).

22   Deepak Chopra, *Seven Spiritual Laws of Success* (San Rafael, CA: Amber-Allen Publishing and New World Library, 1994).

23   For more about planning and scheduling, see "Get a Grip on Time" in Power Position Your Agency, www.korsgaden.com/products/store/

24   Compiled from various sources by the President's Council on Fitness, Sport and Nutrition, www.fitness.gov/resource-center/facts-and-statistics/

25   Statistics reported in "The Toll of Sleep Loss in America," WebMD, www.webmd.com/sleep-disorders/features/toll-of-sleep-loss-in-america

26   "Chronic Disease and Health Promotion," Centers for Disease Control and Prevention, www.cdc.gov/chronicdisease/overview/index.htm

27   See 1 Kings 17:1—19:18.

28   Jack Kinder, Jr. and Garry Kinder with Val Ivanov, *Building the Master Agency* (Erlanger, KY: National Underwriter Company, 2002), p. 11.

29   Cited by Diane Gilbert Madsen in *Hunting for Hemingway* (Woodbury, MN: Midnight Ink, 2010), p. 32.

30   Samuel R. Chand, *Leadership Pain* (Nashville: Thomas Nelson, 2015), p. 195.

31   A statement by St. Basil, cited by Philip Yancey in *Reaching for the Invisible God* (Grand Rapids: Zondervan, 2001), p. 69.

32   For more on specialization, see my booklet *Specialization: The Master Key to Agency Transformation.*

33   Don Martin, *Team Think* (New York: Plume Publishing, 1993).

34   For more about recruiting, interviewing, hiring, onboarding, and supervising staff teams, see *Power Position Your Agency*, pp. 13–33.

35 "Spiritual Disciplines in a Postmodern World," Luci Shaw with Dallas Willard, Radix, Vol. 27, No. 2. Online at www.dwillard.org/articles/artview.asp?artid=56

36 Michael Gerber, *The E-Myth* (New York: HarperBusiness, 1990).

ACKNOWLEDGEMENTS

The completion of any book is a milestone for an author. For me, this book is a work that has been in process for more than fifty years. During this time, I've had my share of successes, but I've also had plenty of difficulties. Through it all, my family has been a constant source of comfort, wisdom, and encouragement. I wouldn't be where I am in life today without them, and I couldn't have written this book without their support. I'm more grateful to them than they'll ever know.

When work on this book began, a friend recommended I talk to Pat Springle to help me craft the message. It has been a pleasure to work with this gifted writer.

HOW TO LEAD A TEAM DISCUSSION ON *SUCCESS & SANITY*

This book is designed for group discussion as well as individual reflection. Many team leaders are looking for material they can use to create more cohesive relationships and clarify the goals of the team. This book includes insights and practical applications to help people achieve more success, but at the same time, find more peace and purpose than ever before.

Let me offer a few suggestions:

- Order enough copies for each person to have a copy of the book. Each week, assign the next chapter and ask people to answer the questions at the end of the chapter before coming to the staff meeting.

- Allot at least twenty minutes for discussion each week, and if the conversation is especially meaningful, consider spending an extra week on that particular chapter.

- Many people underline or highlight passages they find helpful, or they put question marks or other notes in the margins. You might begin by asking people to glance at the chapter and share the points that stand out to them.

- Then go through the questions. You may not have time to discuss all of them, so pick out the ones that promise the best interaction. Later, if you have time, you can ask the ones you bypassed.

- At the end of each discussion, summarize the main principles from the chapter, and ask people to share one application they want to make. If each person makes one application every week, their lives will radically change!

The nature of this book invites self-discovery, and discussions about the chapters invite self-disclosure. Be careful not to go too deep too soon. As the leader, model appropriate self-disclosure. Your team will probably follow your lead. If you sense resistance from a team member, you might have a conversation later to find out what's going on. Or if someone is too open about a sensitive personal issue and it makes others uncomfortable, you may want to set some limits of sharing in the group.

Over the course of the study, however, you can expect everyone in the group to let down their guards to some degree. Most will be very supportive and encouraging to others in the group, but a few may feel very threatened by any discussion of motives, stress, or coping strategies.

The goal of the team discussions, like the goal of any individual reading the book, is to find a new sense of balance and to uncover a new source of peace and purpose so that every aspect of life, at home and at work, is more meaningful than ever before.

ABOUT THE AUTHOR

Troy Korsgaden is one of the insurance industry's most respected consultants, and a highly sought-after speaker. For more than twenty years he has been motivating and educating agency and carrier audiences, ranging in size from 100 to 3,000. Mr. Korsgaden is the founder of Korsgaden International, a leading insurance carrier consulting firm. He is also is the author of many insurance agency how-to books, including *Power Position Your Agency*, *Profit from Change*, *Unleash the Power of Your Agency*, and *Specialization: The Master Key to Agency Transformation*.

Throughout his career, Mr. Korsgaden has been commissioned to speak before major industry organizations such as GAMA, LIMRA, and NAIFA, and to agents from North America's largest carriers, including Allstate, State Farm, Nationwide, American Family, Farmers, Cooperators of Canada, and RBC. He has spoken to more than 150,000 insurance executives, brokers, agents, and staff.

Mr. Korsgaden is also the very successful founder and co-owner of the Korsgaden/Jansma Insurance Agency, which he took from infancy to one of the top Farmers Insurance agencies in North America. With his agency's success, Mr. Korsgaden was the first agent to receive the Lifetime Achievement Award from Farmers Insurance Group of Companies. Some of his many other industry awards include:

- Commercial Agent of the Year, Farmers Insurance Group, 2010-2011

- Perennial Million Dollar Round Table Qualifier

- Presidents Council Member (among the top one-half of one percent of the more than 14,000 U.S. Farmers agents) for 21 consecutive years

- Multiple Agent of the Year Award, Farmers Insurance Group, from among 14,000 agents nationwide

- Personal Lines Agent of the Year, Farmers Insurance Group, from among 14,000 agents nationwide

- Winner, Small Business of the Year, Visalia, California

- Preferred Underwriting Agent

- Multiple Industry Awards and Recognition

Mr. Korsgaden and his family reside in his hometown of Visalia, California.

RESOURCES

For anyone who wants to sell more insurance using better systems and less effort, Troy Korsgaden has developed a library of success tools that will jump-start your agency's growth and help you sustain it over time. Speaking at seminars and through is consulting services, Troy has spent years teaching multi-line insurance agents to grow their businesses. Now his expertise is available to you in the comfort of your own home or office.

He offers a robust set of coaching tools, including books, training videos, handouts, and downloadable forms. All come with Troy's promise to you: if you start implementing what you learn here, you will have a more profitable business in less than a year.

BOOKS

Power Position Your Agency
A Guide to Insurance Agency Success

Are you working too many hours for too few Clients? Does it seem that you do more paperwork than people-work? Will you spend more hours on the road than in front of people this year? Whether your agency is big or small, if you answered yes to any of those questions, you need more than an adrenaline boost! You need sustainable strategies to put you on the path to success.

Troy's best-selling book will teach you:

- How to get appointments with 10 clients every day.

- How to find qualified clients and get them to come to you.

- How to get clients in and out of your office in 30 minutes – or less.

(Visit Korsgaden.com for downloadable purchase)

Profit From Change
Retooling Your Agency for Maximum Profits

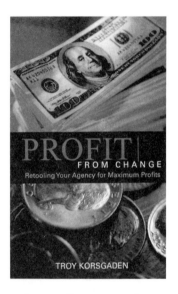

No one knows better than you just how dramatically change has altered the insurance landscape in the last many years. Opportunities to capitalize on those changes and maximize your profits are already within your reach – if you know where to look. This book will help you retool your thinking and strategies to do that. Learn from Troy how to mine the gold that's already in your customer database, turn every product and every employee into a profit center, seize new profits with financial service products, and more. Embrace the future by learning and implementing these simple strategies today.

(Visit Korsgaden.com for downloadable purchase)

Specialization

The Master Key to Agency Transformation

Troy learned early in his career the importance of organizational structure in positioning his agency for success. In the pages of this small but impactful book, he shares insights into how to transform your agency from a generalized agency, to a specialist agency, with employees who are well equipped to meet the needs of your clients. Learn how to grow all lines of insurance, extending far beyond the traditional channels!

(Visit Korsgaden.com for downloadable purchase)

The Unleashed Series

Unleash the Power of Your Agency Workbook & Video Training

In this series, Troy will teach you how to evaluate your business and create a vision for the future – ultimately achieving success that you never dreamed was possible. This comprehensive online training video and corresponding digital download workbook offers a step-by-step guide for growth, and is your ultimate insurance agency business-planning tool. Your purchase includes 12-month access to the Unleashed 5-part video series as well as an accompanying downloadable workbook.

(Visit Korsgaden.com to stream series or download the Executive Workbook in PDF.)

KORSGADEN INTERNATIONAL CARRIER CONSULTING

Distribution

The insurance industry is rapidly changing. New distribution channels are surfacing and quickly becoming competitors for traditional agencies. Every insurer must decide where their agency forces fit into the evolving landscape, and develop tactics to set themselves apart. Troy draws on his thirty years of insurance industry expertise to work alongside carrier organizations to develop strategies which allow them to thrive, even in an uncertain market.

Marketing

Proactive marketing programs can help drastically improve sales and retention, and Insurance companies of all sizes need to focus on creating systems that get results. For the past twenty years, Korsgaden International has been helping the nation's largest carriers implement marketing and retention programs to ensure their agencies' success through Dual Marketing and emphasis on Increased Agency Production. Through a blend of strategy and practical steps, keep your agency running at peak productivity!

IT Consulting

Korsgaden International offers a suite of technology solutions to help organizations measure the effectiveness of marketing efforts and the profitability of sales people:

- Lead generation & management

- Sales automation

- Sales force tracking & measurement

- Analytics

These tools help organizations improve the processes of acquiring new business, retaining customers, managing staff and distributing business resources.

Training

Korsgaden International specializes in helping insurance carriers improve the productivity of their agency distribution systems, and spurring carrier growth by teaching agencies to increase retention and productivity. Training programs are designed to help your agencies operate at maximum productivity and profitability, because the companies we work with understand that agency growth means carrier growth.

Recruiting

An insurance company is only as good as its agencies, and an agency is only as good as its agents and staff. Korsgaden International helps corporations set up recruiting and training systems so that agents know how to bring on the right staff and set them up for success. By utilizing recruiting, onboarding and productivity enhancing systems designed by the Korsgaden International team, you will be able to easily track and improve your return on investment.

To learn more about Korsgaden International and how to access these resources, visit us online at www.korsgaden.com.

SEMINARS & SPEAKING

Troy Korsgaden

Troy is an author and the founder of Korsgaden International & Korsgaden/Jansma Insurance Agency. He is one of the industry's most

highly sought-after platform speakers and trainers for live seminars and events. While his expertise, industry knowledge and ability to teach are unmatched, it is his energy, dynamism, humor and distinctive ability to connect with his audience, which truly set him apart and keep him in demand.

Troy speaks about the most critical components of running a successful, growing business or insurance agency. He offers audiences insights into the programs responsible for his agency's unprecedented results year after year. Frequently addressed topics include:

- Evaluating your business
- Staff recruiting and development
- Retooling your agency
- Finding and retaining customers
- Creating a business roadmap to the future
- Leveraging technology
- Value-selling vs. price-selling
- Cross-selling
- Marketing
- Annual review programs
- Data mining

Troy's no-nonsense methodology and down-to-earth style make him uniquely approachable, allowing business owners and agents to absorb what they learn and instantly apply it for immediate results.

Sharon Jansma

Sharon is the co-founder of Korsgaden/Jansma Insurance Agency. Born and raised in Visalia, California, Sharon grew up with friends, teach-

ers, and mentors who were personally invested in her success and the success of her family. Now leading a thriving business in the town where she was raised, Sharon understands, more than ever, the importance of being connected to community. She explains, "Ultimately, family relationships and close friendships are what bring value and quality of life. It's a constant battle to maintain balance to-day because we are pulled in so many directions."

Having built a successful business while raising a healthy family, Sharon seeks to impart her wisdom and experiences to other agents and business owners who wish to enjoy both success and joy in all areas of life. She relates, "With every decision we make—whether it's financial, emotional, professional, spiritual or personal—we've got to weigh the costs. We have to decide what fits with what we are trying to achieve. Balance is a daily task."

Sharon specializes in speaking to groups on challenging and inspiring topics, including:

Agency Management—Writing new business, retaining customers and consistently giving them an excellent experience, navigating financial and insurance responsibilities, and casting vision while living in the present.

Staffing—Hiring the right people, managing and growing a team, cultivating a healthy work environment, and creating a professional space where you and your staff enjoy coming to work each day.

Practicing Presence—Compartmentalization and the art of being fully present, whether you are at work or at home, and developing a well-balanced life.

The Value of Mentorship—Recognizing you will always have room to grow and learn, seeking help from experts in all areas of life, and making yourself available to those who can benefit from what you know.

Contact us at www.korsgaden.com
to book Troy or Sharon at your next event!